CHINA WATCH

CHINA WATCH

John King Fairbank

Harvard University Press

Cambridge, Massachusetts
and London, England
1987

This book is printed on acid-free paper, and its binding materials
have been chosen for strength and durability.

Set in Linotron Sabon and designed by Marianne Perlak

Library of Congress Cataloging-in-Publication Data
Fairbank, John King, 1907–
China watch.

Includes index.
1. China—History—1949– . 2. China—
Relations—United States. 3. United States—Relations—
China. I. Title.
DS777.55.F25   1987   951.05   86-33570
ISBN 0-674-11765-4 (alk. paper)

To the memory
of the top reporter
THEODORE H. WHITE
(1915–1986)

PREFACE

Recently China has come alive and turned toward us. What does this mean for our future? China-watchers fresh out of business school applaud China's belated conversion to the market and the profit motive that they say make America tick. Looking ahead, others anticipate that a modernized China may soon start doing to us on a bigger scale what the Japanese have been doing to us in recent years—excelling us in technology and underselling us in the world market. Along this line of thought, the Chinese may eventually be supplying our clothing and household appliances while we sell them our farm surplus.

But can China actually become another Japan? To think so may be still another American dream about the sleeping giant and about the vast China trade that we have constantly foreseen but never found. Perhaps the same difficulties that have so delayed China's entrance into modern times will continue to slow her progress.

The potential riches of trade with China have been part of our westward-facing dreamworld for two hundred years. Our image of China has had a long history. We are just beginning to realize that the image has been a filtrate of reality, accumulated through our preconceptions as well as our contacts. Both have shaped the reports of China-watchers.

This volume incorporates one historian-observer's writings on China and Chinese-American relations over the last fifteen years. Plainly I am part of that evanescent but important phenomenon, the formation of public opinion. Authors react to historical personalities and events in or concerning China when they write books, articles, and reviews; they give their own impressions or comment on the impressions of others. Soon realities and images merge.

What does this double filtration represent—this writing about the reactions of others? We know that the publishers of the books and the editors of the reviewing journals and newspapers each had to decide whether the books were worth publishing or reviewing in the first place. Many judgments were involved, from many angles; and so, perhaps, the contents of this volume can tell us something about what has interested a portion of the American public that reads and even thinks about China. Some, especially if they like the contents, can feel that these pages represent public opinion. Granted that this representation would be tendentious, fragmented, and indecisive, it might still compete with public-opinion surveys.

The Introduction (taken in part from an address at the centenary meeting of the American Historical Association in December 1985) reflects my interest in how the various American attitudes toward China have accumulated. Each of the five parts begins with a historical context. Some chapters too begin with notes written from today's vantage point; others are reprinted virtually as first published.

CONTENTS

CHINA WATCH

The Growth of Chinese History in American Minds

It is hard enough to understand ourselves, and of course even harder to understand a distant people like the Chinese with their different history and culture. The attempt, however, still must be made—and perhaps we are even gaining on the situation.

Take, for example, the new American religion of human rights. It is more culture bound than we think. Human rights will not become a dominant doctrine in China until China becomes as legalistic a society as America, which is not likely to happen for a long time. This is because, stated briefly, rights and duties are the respective residues of Christianity and Confucianism. The result is a contrast between the ideals of individual striving and of collective harmony, motifs that come down from three thousand years of history and are not easily expungable.

For example, the American concern for the individual has been expressed legally in the question of intent. Willfully causing a death is murder, but causing a death accidentally and without malice aforethought may be classed as homicide and deserve a different penalty. Not so in the old China. Lack of intent was not a mitigating factor in judging a crime. The classic case is that of an American sailor with the remarkably felicitous name of Terranova, who in 1821 dropped a jar overboard that struck a bumboat woman, who fell into the water and was drowned. In order to keep their trade going at Canton, the American merchants handed Terranova over to Chinese justice, which according to Chinese law very properly had him strangled in no time. Such examples led to the system of extraterritoriality that was given fullest expression in the first Chinese-American treaty of 1844. For a century afterward, until the unequal treaties were abolished in 1943, extraterritoriality (or the jurisdiction of American consular officers in

1

China over Americans and their property there) was the backbone of the treaty system. It gave the Americans in China a special privileged status, but it also prevented a lot of ill feeling.

In brief, the right of extraterritoriality that the British and the rest of us claimed in China in the age of imperialism was a concrete expression of what we now call human rights. The present is linked with the past more than we realize. So it is with other major motifs in Chinese-American relations—the great American expectations of an enormous trade with China, which so far has never materialized; the inveterate missionary impulse to give the Chinese the best in our culture, which in the case of Christian missions produced many important good works but few converts. In the Chinese-American relationship we keep trying to express our cultural values while the Chinese respond with theirs. To prepare for our unknown but rapidly approaching future with China, we may well take note of the American image of China that has developed through historic stages.

This image is of course a very slippery subject, the creation in the first instance of the American China pundits, that mixed crew of travelers, missionaries, journalists, consuls, businessmen, students, and tourists who tell their fellow citizens all about it. The resulting image is at best a kaleidoscope that combines discordant views and keeps on constantly changing. Efforts to describe this image of China accumulate from textbooks, memoirs, novels, movies, and radio-television events and commentaries. Yet out of all this confusion each generation of Americans seems to derive a broadly accepted view, at least among those worthy citizens who make it a practice to have views. The successive stages of a scheme of periodization may give us perspective.

In the two hundred years of our relations with China the American understanding had to grow up from zero. We began by inheriting the European view of China, which was that of the Enlightenment of the eighteenth century. As late as the British and Dutch embassies to Peking in the 1790s, the minuscule American impression of China, the land that had after all provided the tea for the Boston Tea Party in 1773, was still in the shadow of the Enlightenment's enthusiasm. The early missionary prowess in what we now call public relations had been demonstrated by the Jesuits, whose reports, under the titillating title of *Lettres édifiantes et cu-*

rieuses, were widely circulated. They portrayed China in the ideal terms that suffuse the Confucian classics and filled the minds of the Jesuits' Chinese informants, who had all been turned out by the thought factory of the classical examination system. The emperor's preternatural wisdom and benevolence (except when he had you bastinadoed for having wrong ideas) was matched by the wealth and well-being of the people, whose living standard as a matter of fact still compared quite well with that of Europeans. The savants of the Enlightenment used the Jesuits' idealized reports of China to show that you could be quite civilized even without the overrated benefit of revealed religion. But the Enlightenment's image of China was abstract, esoteric, and unreal.

A phase of disillusionment set in from more direct contact in the early nineteenth century, coupled with the West's material progress at home. In the eighteenth century European chamber pots might be emptied in the gutter, whereas China already had a night-soil collection and disposal system of nutritional benefit. But when piped water and the water closet came into vogue in the West, China was left behind. By the time the China trade gave Westerners direct contact with the steamy ordure of Canton, China was rapidly becoming "backward," lacking in steam engines, artillery, and other sinews of civilization. Never mind that law reform, policemen, and hospitals were recent developments in the West; it had the lead in those two engines of modern history, science and nationalism, and China even today is still busy catching up.

Thus the dreamworld China of the eighteenth century was rudely supplanted by sordid backwardness. Once Protestant revivalism began to send American missionaries to the heathen, it could be asserted that industry, democracy, and Christianity were the trinity that produced Western power. If Chinese scholar-officials thought they knew better, they had no way to prove it. The gunboat was a decisive fact, and the high-principled missionary could not be kept out.

The period of contact and disillusion in the first half of the nineteenth century produced an all-around and very informative work on China by a missionary printer, S. Wells Williams: *The Middle Kingdom,* a two-volume work subtitled *A survey of the geography, government, education, social life, arts, religion, etc. of the Chinese empire and its inhabitants* (1848). The 1883 revised and enlarged edition was subtitled a bit differently, as *A survey of the geography, government, literature, social life, arts and history, etc. of the Chinese empire and its inhabitants.* This widely read work was the great-grandfather of what is now called area study, posited on the recognition that a different civilization must be studied as a whole and from all angles. In describing China, language, history, society, and culture could never be disentangled. The amalgam became known as sinology.

The Middle Kingdom combined two things. The first was the early China-coast sinology of the pioneer Anglo-American missionaries, which had accumulated after 1832 in the *Chinese Repository,* the journal the missionaries put out in Macao and Canton. Second, the book incorporated Williams' direct observation of China's premodern problems, which confirmed in him and his readers the conviction that the Chinese people needed not only the steam engine and plumbing of Western material civilization, but also the spiritual teaching of Jesus Christ. Here, in short, was enshrined the expansive American Christian formula: "We have it, they lack it, we ought to give it to them so that they can be more like us and pursue our ideals." In the 1980s we Americans are still seeking to give the Chinese people both our scientific technology, including social science, and our doctrine of individualism focused on human rights. It is plain that for all our progress we have not got far beyond the values and underlying attitudes of Williams' *Middle Kingdom.* In short, the history of China in American minds shows a high degree of continuity on the level of cultural values.

Williams' all-about-China book of 1848 had many successors, including Kenneth Scott Latourette's *The Chinese: Their History and Culture* of 1934 and other works too numerous to mention. By Latourette's time the modern study of Chinese classics and history had led to more scholarly results, but the high drama of China's ancient glory and modern inferiority seemed to stand out from the record, as it does even today. We could rejoice in the fact that it was the British, not we, who had used gunboats to secure our privilege of extraterritoriality. The British had also kept us out of their India-to-China opium trade. Our record impressed us as utterly benevolent. With China we felt we had a benign "special relationship." We were unaware that China's policy was to cultivate a special relationship with all foreign invaders, just in case.

The nineteenth-century disillusionment with China was capped by another widely read book, *Chinese Characteristics,* by the Reverend Arthur H. Smith, who had spent many years in a Shantung village trying to Christianize China from the bottom up and also observing Chinese ways at the village level. Written as a series of essays in the 1880s, *Chinese Characteristics* was published in 1894 and became a classic account of Chinese life as seen from the viewpoint of middle America. The book also marked a new phase as the most eye-catching account of social differences, the basis for later sociological analysis. Smith highlighted both "poverty" and "social solidarity" as cultural differences. The formal study of sociology began in China in the 1900s.

Meanwhile, foundations were laid for the study of imperialism in China. Western privileges claimed and enforced under the unequal treaty system had been enlarged in a series of wars. By the twentieth century the legal structure of these privileges had become a labyrinth of interlocking arrangements. Their provenance was recounted in H. B. Morse's *International Relations of the Chinese Empire,* volume 1 dated 1910 and volumes 2 and 3, 1918. After thirty-three years of working for the Chinese government as an imperial maritime customs commissioner, Morse had had a wide experience of Chinese official life. His summary of how the foreign position had become established provided a baseline for study of the unequal treaty system until its demise in 1943.

In brief, the twentieth century began a new phase in the American attitude toward China, a non-Western civilization, as a subject of study. In this gradually expanding twentieth-century effort both the ideal image of the Enlightenment and the disillusioned image of the nineteenth century have contributed to a repertoire of ways to understand China, both the good and the bad, from the American cultural point of view. Well-established stereotypes have become available, which may be called upon to shape the American attitude at any given time. The continuing fluctuations of this approach can be illustrated in recent history.

As a first example, take the anti-imperialist Boxer Rebellion of 1900, which produced the worst hostage crisis of the nineteenth century. In that long, hot summer fanatical Boxer rebels, backed by the Manchu dynasty, besieged 475 foreign civilians plus 450 military of eight nations, about 3,000 Chinese Christians and 150 racing ponies (which were soon eaten) in the Peking Legation quarter. Because the European nations still had their concert of powers ready to tolerate one another's imperialisms, there was no danger of superpower confrontation. The Russians simply took over Manchuria, from which the Japanese did not dislodge them until the Russo-Japanese War of 1904–1905, after which the Japanese had to be classified as white men pushing to the fore of international life. After the Peking Legations were rescued by troops from all the major nations, the Boxers disappeared back into the countryside while the Manchu dynasty was preserved in order to keep China at peace, which would facilitate foreign trade. The American image of China as of 1900 was one of heathen barbarism, quite inferior to the civilization of Europe, which had not yet gone over the cliff into World War I.

Yet paradoxically the 1900 crisis gave birth to the American Open Door doctrine, which not only claimed access to China on a me-too basis but also sought to preserve China's opportunity to develop as a modern nation-state. These mixed motifs of a barbarian backwardness and a nationalist striving for modernity were interwoven in the American image of China during the first half of the twentieth century. A decade after the Boxer crisis Americans generally welcomed the advent in 1911 of the Chinese Republic, blandly assuming that China was going to be a Christian republic like ourselves. We deplored the political chaos of the warlord era, but meanwhile fostered the growth of a dozen Christian colleges. Increasingly we supported China against Japanese encroachment. When Japan, through its Twenty-one Demands of 1915, tried to consolidate its special position in China, hoping thereby to surpass the Western imperialists, American opinion took China's side. At the end of World War I in 1919, when the peace settlement let Japan retain the imperialist position it had seized from Germany in Shantung province, we refused to ratify the treaty. For the next thirty years, until 1949, we more and more backed the Republic of China against Japan's aggression.

Yet the yo-yo-like fluctuations in the American attitude continued to dominate the American image of China.

When the Kuomintang (KMT) under Chiang Kai-shek came to power in the Nanking government of 1928–1937, foreigners both in and out of China had high hopes that it would begin to meet China's urgent problems. Unfortunately, by the time the KMT came to power, it had turned its back on its Chinese Communist allies. It killed those it could get hold of in the cities and forced the survivors like Mao Tse-tung out into the boondocks. After 1931 the aggression of Japanese militarism led to China's final militarization and its clamping down on social revolution.

Forcing revolutionary intellectuals to live among peasants created an explosive mixture, however. By the time Pearl Buck's best-seller *The Good Earth* (1931) brought Chinese peasants onto the American public horizon, Mao and his colleagues were learning how to mobilize them for political power. A young Kansas City journalist, Edgar Snow, put out Mao's story in *Red Star over China* (1937). *Red Star* wrote the handwriting on the wall for us to see.

But America's bread was buttered on the KMT side. We could do business with Chiang Kai-shek, though he gave us a rather low return on our investment. Disillusionment came in the 1940s when Chiang and the KMT proved quite unable to mobilize support against the Communist takeover.

In a similar fashion the Chinese Communist Party (CCP), when in the boondocks at Yenan during World War II, had shown foreign observers such admirable qualities that many China specialists viewed it as a hopeful development. Disillusion shortly supervened, when the People's Republic seemed to become part of Mr. Dulles' "monopolistic, atheistic communism," a worldwide conspiracy directed from Moscow. Having no peasants ourselves, we felt that only Moscow, home of the antichrist, could produce such a big movement. The cold-war era may be described as a totalitarian phase in American perceptions. In the 1950s some deplored the bad way the CCP had harassed and killed so many of its Chinese enemies, while others extolled the good way it had cleaned the place up, both liberating the peasants and making the trains run on time.

During the resumption of Sino-American diplomatic relations in the 1970s the good impression that China made on the early American observers was soon followed by the bad impression created when we learned of the horrible excesses of the Cultural Revolution. By the time normalization of relations was achieved in 1979, Mao Tse-tung and his faction had left the scene; a new era was dawning with the usual resurgence of American hope and tourist enthusiasm for the People's Republic of China.

One could go on noting how events in China continued to

trigger moralistic stereotypes that expressed our cultural values. American attitudes toward the Chinese people have been strongly value laden ever since we reneged on our treaty promise of mutual immigration and in the 1880s excluded Chinese from the United States.

One thing we know about the Chinese people today is that their attitude toward us is even more righteous than our attitude toward them. Or is it? Take the controversy over abortion. To avoid starvation-suffocation from numbers (1.24 billion or so by the year 2000), the People's Republic tries to permit only one child per couple. By aiming so high, the hope is actually to get down to a birth ratio of 1.7, which will still see an increase because so many are young, but will eventually stabilize the cancerous population growth. What else can the Chinese do? As part of the effort, abortion is made available.

Yet they find their American friends in the throes of a new cult, the adoration of the fetus (never mind the mother). This is on a par with the Virgin Birth, which the Chinese heard about in the nineteenth century but didn't buy. What are the Chinese to make of such sincere righteousness from the Americans?

We can only hope that the radical extremists in our two countries never join forces, denying a woman her human right to choose. The Chinese extremists want to compel her to abort, the American extremists want to compel her not to. The extremists have something in common, and could no doubt bring themselves to fight each other in defense of their rather similar, though opposed, principles. Between the American claims of the absolute sanctity of fetal life before birth and the Chinese claims to the overriding precedence of the needs of society over those of the individual, women could have a problem.

As in the other cases of culture conflict noted in the following chapters, both sides would do well to study each other's history and find out how their opponents became so misguided. Meantime the moderate majorities in the two countries have to go on living together.

In this enterprise I think one guiding principle may be worth putting forward. In our rational analyses of other peoples' revolutions, we Americans often slight one essential component. That is the compelling ideal or vision of the leaders, by which they move their followers. It happens that China's revolution has been moti-vated by two such visions: first, that of the patriot who wants to see a new China standing tall and proud among the nations; sec-ond, that of uplifting the underprivileged peasant masses to sur-mount the ancient upper-class/lower-class bifurcation of the soci-ety. At any given time during the revolutionary process these two visions have competed for attention.

Most of us can appreciate the first, materialistic vision of a strong modern nation more easily than the second, social one. This is no doubt because we ourselves have gone far to achieve the former but have seldom confronted the latter as an urgent, all-encompassing problem.

How does one bring the great mass of China's peasantry into the life of culture, public service, and profit that China's highly educated upper class so long enjoyed? In order to achieve this vast enterprise, even though the Chinese have a stronger sense of com-mon cultural identity than most peoples, they face the need to create new social values and new political institutions. This vision underlay the dragonlike thrashing about of Chairman Mao. In a more practical, less strenuous form it also motivates the recent reforms under Deng Xiaoping. In the case studies that follow, all these motifs are illustrated.

PART ONE

New Views of Imperialism

The Marxist-Leninist outlook adopted in the Chinese Revolution since 1949 (after thirty years of gestation from 1919) has paradoxically brought Chinese and American views of the world closer together. We are now able to argue, for example, over the forms and nature of Western imperialism in China. We have, at least, more vocabulary in common. That we should have opposing views of imperialism is only natural, given the fact that our experiences of it were in such contrast on the giving and receiving sides. In a pale imitation of the British in India, we enjoyed our superior status in a semicolonial China, whereas Chinese patriots were less enthused.

Today, however, researchers are getting at the details of the imperialist era. On the whole, I think we can conclude that Lenin's type of economic imperialism, depending on the circumstances, was almost as much a help as a hindrance to China's economic development, whereas on the political-psychological plane foreign aggression was a humiliation that aroused Chinese nationalism and fomented the great Chinese Revolution of the twentieth century.

The term "imperialism" has of course been ambiguous in American thinking. As first used in the nineteenth century, it referred to the European powers extending their political control over other peoples in the regions where those peoples lived. In short, it meant colonialism. But at the end of the nineteenth century, Lenin and others, inspired partly by the new science of economics, saw the real evil as capitalist or financial imperialism, which might enslave a people from abroad without necessarily taking them over as a colony.

Americans at the turn of the century remained well aware that the United States had not participated in the colonial imperialism of the European powers. Our substitute for the Europeans' taking over of certain areas of China as their special enclaves was to assert the principle of the open door for trade. This "me-too" policy was a substitute for, or at least an alternative to, genuine imperialism. The "integrity of China" that we espoused in the Open Door doctrine of 1900 was a further gesture leaving us free of imperialist contamination. Only after World War I did the Leninist idea come to the fore, and then the Americans were able to reject it, because unlike the British in India we were not at all dependent on our trade with China. In fact that trade remained quite small. In the end, capitalist imperialism has not served as a convenient description of American policy toward China. Our fighting the Japanese 1941–1945 and then fighting in Korea 1950–1953 and in Vietnam 1965–1973 are more easily classified under power politics pure and simple. Our stake in these wars was not primarily economic.

This fact makes our warfare all the more ominous, because power politics and its accompanying militarism seem likely to continue as long as nationalism continues, no matter what the economic system may be. The Reagan administration's view of anti-communism as equivalent to "freedom," which must be defended militarily, illustrates this myopic response to situations of power politics rivalry. We need to remember that greed has seldom fueled warfare as powerfully as idealism.

Our imperialism toward China thus boils down essentially to a phenomenon of expansion. We have been more expansionist than most modern nation-states. Expansion, however, is a rather neutral term, not necessarily good or bad, which can characterize both our government policy and our private missionary movement.

1

The Motive Power of Opium

In the People's Republic modern times begin in 1840 with the Opium War—mostly a British operation, the *locus classicus* for profit-seeking aggression. With such an opening to set the tone of Sino-Western contact, China's half-dozen later wars against assorted imperialists have seemed to most Chinese simply like more of the same. Now that the American century of friendship and unequal treaty privileges in China has been followed by our Korean and Vietnam wars, scholars are taking a closer look at Western imperialism as a basic fact of China's experience. Our predecessors a century ago, though they lacked our firepower, did the best they could with new side-wheel gunboats like Britain's *Nemesis*. Better still, they knew what they wanted—the profits of trade—which in those days coincided with the spread of civilization.

The opium trade from India to China was the longest-continued systematic international crime of modern times, but the responsibility for it was so diffused that it went on for more than a hundred years, constantly paying its way. Opium was manufactured in India and sold at periodic auctions by the British Indian government. The private merchants who took it to China were simply middle-

Part of this chapter appeared in the *New York Times Book Review,* January 11, 1976, as a review of Peter Ward Fay, *The Opium War, 1840–1842: Barbarians in the Celestial Empire in the Early Part of the Nineteenth Century and the War by Which They Forced Her Gates Ajar* (Chapel Hill: University of North Carolina Press, 1975; Cambridge: Cambridge University Press, 1975), and of Jack Beeching, *The Chinese Opium Wars* (New York: Harcourt Brace Jovanovich, 1975). Copyright © 1976 by the New York Times Company. Reprinted by permission.

men transporting it to the coast, where Chinese smugglers took delivery. The big Chinese distribution network, unresearched thus far, exploited a demand that grew up in China after 1800 along with overpopulation, hard times, and corruption.

At first China had few addicts, but by the late nineteenth century it had millions and millions, and its own opium production rivaled that of India. Opium addiction was particularly disastrous for the old Chinese way of life, because Confucianism set such great store by self-discipline and duty to family, whereas the opium addict had to satisfy his own craving first and sacrifice his family as well as himself. The moral issue of the opium trade was recognized by both sides from the start. Half a dozen times humanitarian efforts in Parliament brought the issue to a vote, but never brought the trade to an end until 1917.

Consider first motives. Despite all Prime Minister Palmerston's rhetoric demanding freedom of trade and access, diplomatic equality, and the protection of English law for Englishmen, the really compelling motive was money—primarily from opium sales and taxes in India, and then from the tea duties in Britain on a tea trade largely financed by opium sales at Canton.

Look second at the wherewithal for waging the war. The *casus belli* was the confinement of the British at Canton when Commissioner Lin Tse-hsu tried to stamp out opium in 1839. The plans for the campaign and Britain's war aims came to Palmerston directly from leading British free-traders like Dr. William Jardine, who was also the chief opium merchant. Vessels of the opium fleet were hired to help carry the expeditionary forces from India. Opium ship captains were employed as pilots, opium firm translators as interpreters. The expedition's military and diplomatic leaders benefited from the opium traders' hospitality and advice; the quartermaster got his funds by selling bills (cashing checks) on London banks in exchange for silver acquired from Chinese buyers at the opium receiving stations along the coast. From the beginning it was intended that a Chinese indemnity should pay the full costs of the expedition. The war was really a speculation expected to pay for itself and also to make indirect profits. Its outcome was the defeat of the ruling Ch'ing dynasty and the 1842 Treaty of Nanking, which called for the then-enormous indemnity to the British of $21 million.

In the context of the times the Opium War was overshadowed in the British press by the Afghan War and the reconquest of Kabul, which were of more immediate concern to the Indian empire. Opium had invaded Britain, its victims including not only the famous Thomas De Quincy and Samuel Taylor Coleridge, who consumed quarts of laudanum mixture, but also William Wilberforce, the reform leader. Some five hundred chests of opium a year came into England for English addicts, while twenty thousand—and eventually eighty thousand—went to China. The humanitarian concern expressed by the young Gladstone about the opium trade was later muted amid outcries about the growing evils of Britain's industrialization. The trade came to an end in World War I largely because the market was then preempted by Chinese producers in China.

One unresolved moral dimension of this story was faced by the Protestant missionaries, who abhorred opium but sympathized with the war, and the Catholic missionaries, who were simultaneously expanding their own secret and subversive activities in the Chinese interior. Catholic missions were an integral part of the invasion. These less visible spiritual entrepreneurs traveled through the provinces in disguise, sheltered by secret Christian communities, to maintain a heterodox cult in the midst of the decaying empire. French priests, who met martyrdom in central China, defied the Chinese establishment just as explicitly as did opium trader Jardine and his partner, Alexander Matheson, on the coast. Even Catholic priests, when they traveled, to say nothing of Protestants, often had to take advantage of the transportation and financing provided by the opium traders. That the Western invasion was all of a piece will certainly become the established wisdom.

Indeed, the opening of China, even in accounts of the Western side of it, emerges more sharply as a joint Sino-foreign venture. The Chinese catechumens of the Lazarists and Jesuits, who helped maintain the small Christian community, were systemic counterparts to the tea compradores and Chinese opium distributors in the Sino-foreign trade. The basic rule of foreign activity in China was that nothing really could be done without Chinese assistance. Beginning with the Chinese demand for opium rather than Lancashire textiles, and continuing with the enormous opium distribution network in Chinese hands beyond foreign purview, the opium trade from its inception was a Sino-foreign phenomenon. This Chinese component in the Western invasion was of course composed of desperadoes, opportunists, and dissidents of the worst sort. Hong Kong became a haven for smugglers and secret society men who were outcasts from the Confucian order. China's road to revolution and rebirth led at first distinctly downward, even though Christian missions and the Chinese Christian community eventually emerged in the twentieth century as one of the finest and most patriotic sectors of a new China.

In the 1840s one repeatedly sees the hand of the opium merchant guiding the diplomats and assisting the military. Chinese officials made repeated efforts to catch up with Western military technique, learning from experience and disaster. The finale was the burning of the Summer Palace in 1860, after it had been looted by the invading armies of the British and French. Today's investigative reporting pulls together the sinister and even conspiratorial aspects of the opium trade, the connivance of government with it, and the general immorality of the British invasion despite its high-sounding aims and sanctions.

The iniquities of the old China, in decay throughout the nineteenth century, contrast with the progressive new order of the treaty ports. Thus the chief British representative, Capt. Charles Elliot, who was always stopping the warfare to keep the trade going, deserves some credit for humanitarian, antiopium impulses. The aversion of the British traders to the humane viewpoint of Lord Elgin, who in 1858–1860 dutifully completed the work of "opening" China begun in 1836, is of course better known.

As a social evil with many victims over the years, opium has its latter-day counterparts in drugs like heroin and nicotine. The humanitarian difficulty in stopping British Indian opium production and shipment to China casts light on the current American problem of getting the big cigarette companies to stop manufacturing cigarettes. Having accepted the idea that cigarettes are dangerous to our health, we still find the tobacco interest widely based in states that sometimes have vociferous representatives in Congress. Furthermore, the bondholders of the cigarette firms also have an interest at stake. In short, we find that our current addiction to tobacco has been recognized as an evil for a long time, but tobacco sales help the American economy too much to be given up. If we want to continue throwing stones at British India because of its opium trade, we should save some for ourselves.

2

Missionary and Cowboy Attitudes: America's "Special Relationship" with China

The American sentimentality about China, which so appalled Churchill when he visited Roosevelt in 1941, is still alive in the White House forty-five years later, even though reduced to a residual concern for Taiwan. It is still a special case that challenges historians to explain it. One must begin by putting the United States' China policy in the general context of American conservative wishfulness about today's outside world. American-Soviet rivalry, a white-and-black drama pitting Hollywood against the KGB, brings out the American stereotypes regardless of their utility. Behind Mr. Reagan's playing to his audience of the moment loom the missionary and cowboy attitudes that informed America's transcontinental and trans-Pacific expansion—the righteous exhortation to shape up democratically, but in any case the readiness to support the assumed good guys with firepower.

These culture-bound attitudes of evangelism and righteous violence, so often combined in the American neighborhood, did not at first combine in the special case of China; Victorian Britain did the original dirty work there by fighting for unequal treaty privileges, and so the Americans could enjoy the opportunities of trade and proselytism without the stigma of having secured them by force. This, I think, lay at the heart of the enduring American sentiment about China as an outlet for the Christian impulse unim-

This chapter appeared in the *Times Literary Supplement,* June 24, 1983, as a review of Michael H. Hunt, *The Making of a Special Relationship: The United States and China to 1914* (New York: Columbia University Press, 1983), and of James Reed, *The Missionary Mind and American East Asia Policy, 1911–1915* (Cambridge, Massachusetts: Council on East Asian Studies, Harvard University, 1983).

paired by the onus of coercion. The British navy supplied the gunboats. The Americans could preach. Today Mr. Reagan's atavistic concern for Taiwan, like Mrs. Thatcher's for Hong Kong, echoes the Palmerstonian era when the unequal treaty system was imposed on the Manchu dynasty so that foreign trade with China could prosper under foreign law, and foreigners' human rights in China could be protected by extraterritoriality. Let us not deride our predecessors. Human rights are still a militant issue.

The American warfare in Korea, the Taiwan straits, and Vietnam can be traced back to what Michael Hunt calls "the Open Door constituency," by which he means "a set of interest groups—American businessmen, missionaries, and diplomats—with a common commitment to penetrating China and propagating at home a paternalistic vision of defending and reforming China." The early American profits from opium, tea, and silk in the old Canton trade after 1784 founded the never-realized myth of the China market. After 1830, Protestant missionary pioneers, finding no converts, developed their two-way function as image makers. They told the Chinese of the triune benefits of Christianity, democracy, and material progress, while describing to their home constituents the faded grandeur of a Chinese civilization sinking in decay, sin, and heathenism. The commercial and evangelical interests coalesced by the 1890s in demanding an open door of opportunity to seek Chinese buyers and believers.

This "special relationship" is noteworthy because it was so especially unequal. By midcentury, Cantonese surplus labor had discovered California, and soon the Chinese arriving there greatly outnumbered the Americans going to China. There were curious parallels: the Chinese coolie laborers in the United States and the American missionaries in China were both immigrants and brought their cultures with them. This produced among the local and normally xenophobic populace some "strikingly mirrored anxieties [about] the supposed proclivity of depraved missionary and immigrant alike to defy sexual taboos and to make use of drugs and potions to seduce unwary women and children . . . The mission compound no less than Chinatown was regarded as a hotbed of subversion."

In the 1880s and 1890s, when American missionaries sometimes suffered from mob action in China, Chinese laborers hired to build the western American railways suffered from mob action by American workers. In these parallel but unrelated riots, scores of Chinese died but almost no Americans. The Chinese were only ordinary foreigners, quite lacking in gunboats.

As the American missionary-cum-legation secretary, S. Wells Williams, noted as early as 1868, "If the Americans in China had suffered one tithe of the wrongs that the Chinese have endured within the United States since 1855, there would certainly have been a war on account of it." Sino-American treaties gave reciprocal rights of trade and residence, but the American labor movement, still struggling for its right to exist, denied any such right to Chinese labor. The movement for Chinese exclusion grew steadily in the American West and the open door from the Canton region to California was summarily closed, while the movement in China to get rid of missionaries led only to the futile Boxer rising in 1900, after which the missionaries became more numerous and the Open Door in China became an American shibboleth.

Meanwhile, Chinese statesmen accustomed to utilizing eastern Mongols against western Mongols and vice versa could seldom resist trying to use the Americans to offset the British, Japanese, or Russians. Yet throughout China's long wooing of American good offices, mediation, neutral support, or outright alliance against other powers, the Americans by temperament consistently led the Chinese on to expect more American performance than ever eventuated. Feeling themselves free of the taint of imperialism and honest in their intentions (they had no need for dishonesty), American representatives official and otherwise confided to the Chinese their distrust of the other powers, their devotion to peace and friendship, and their readiness to help. Since the American posture was almost entirely one of talk without any intention of or capacity for Realpolitik, all this friendly flatulence came to nothing and merely misled the Chinese. Time after time, when it came to action, the Americans remained passive.

Take, for example, the efforts of Li Hung-chang to make use of the United States in his hope of warding off disaster by having a foreign policy in Korea. Every time, the American naval officers, diplomats, advisers, or ex-presidents like U. S. Grant proved more quick with words than with useful action. Secretary of State John Hay made a good thing out of the British Open Door idea, but he never bothered to consult the Chinese about it. During the 1900s

Chang Chih-tung and other statesmen trying to save the Northeast (Manchuria) from Russo-Japanese condominium repeatedly turned to the anti-imperialist United States, but never with any success. In these same years the U.S. Bureau of Immigration regularly harassed and humiliated Chinese students, scholars, and even officials seeking to enter the Golden Gate. Hunt exhumes an appalling record of American racist arrogance that in 1905 triggered China's first patriotic boycott movement against American goods.

James Reed begins his study of the so-called Missionary Mind by noting how the American Protestant leaders confused in their thinking the expression of their normative ideals with their appraisals of reality. By the spread of "Christian Civilization" they meant really the spread of the white Protestant Christianity of northern Europe and North America. When they spoke of "Christian China," hope was inextricably mixed with reality. Thus in 1914 the great evangelist Sherwood Eddy, fresh from revival meetings in China, declared, "We have long ceased to doubt that we will win Asia for Christ." In short, the Protestant missions lived on doses of wishful thinking. The British China hand J. O. P. Bland in 1912 saw the American enthusiasm for China's republican revolution as a reflection of "the instinctive American love for the underdog and the reassuring optimism" of the missionary public, "to whom optimism is a vocational necessity."

The hopeful assumptions and indomitable unrealism of this view infected American policy thinking, because the American missionary community was the only part of the country with firsthand information and a definite interest at stake. Assuming that at the turn of the century there were always some three hundred China missionaries on furlough in the United States, Reed estimates that they presented their case in public at least thirty thousand times a year, enough to keep their constituency of perhaps five million Protestant supporters properly concerned. The American business community, meanwhile, found that only 2 percent of American trade was with China. But it had inherited the tradition of the big profits of the old China trade before the Civil War and in the 1890s it was ready to hope for a China market. On the whole, American men of affairs were Europe oriented. The foreign service was not yet a profession, and American interpreters and translators came mainly from missionary sources.

Thus the Missionary Mind formed American opinion by default.

"The campaign for Christian Civilization became a kind of crusade, between the years 1905 and 1915 . . . Thousands of bright young well-scrubbed Protestant Student Volunteers sailed from San Francisco to build a Christian Civilization in Asia . . . By 1915 there were nearly 10,000 foreign missionaries . . . one in every 1500 adult Protestants."

In the absence of large economic and strategic interests, American policymakers were left to conceive of their role in China as benevolent and high principled. This laid them wide open to the Chinese penchant for the cajoling of the foreigner through friendship. Minister Paul S. Reinsch, who almost single-handedly triggered the American protest against Japan's Twenty-one Demands of 1915, did not disclose to the State Department that he was guided every evening by secret consultations with the astute young Wellington Koo of the Chinese foreign office, who depicted the Japanese menace in fervent terms but without disclosing too many details. Koo appealed to the benevolent paternalism of Professor Reinsch and found an eventual response in that other political scientist, Professor Woodrow Wilson, who was then president.

Hunt's Open Door constituency and Reed's Missionary Mind had paternalistic and rather arrogantly aggressive qualities, which both authors see conducing later to the warfare in Korea and Vietnam. The American attitude toward China was unrealistic, misled, writes Reed, by "dangerous good intentions," by a "flawed and essentially ethnocentric vision," writes Hunt. Hunt also observes that "China—vast, populous, and teetering between renovation and collapse—held out boundless opportunity to the American expansionist impulse in all its guises." One could go further and suggest that China represented not only opportunity but a concrete need for help of the sort that missionary good works, and later John D. Rockefeller, could supply. The special relationship had its origin on the Chinese side in the complex strivings that led China into revolution. The ideas of a special relationship and of winning China for Christ were recurrent American responses to China's ever-growing potentiality for modern transformation.

The Chinese culture that came under stress from modern changes was the most distinctive, separate, and ancient, the most self-sufficient, balanced, and massive, of any culture known to history. China's intermittent revolution, fitfully gathering steam during the last hundred fifty years, is therefore by far the most deep-going and large-scale social change ever required by history. American believers in change, dimly aware of this titanic and tortuous process, responded in the various fashions that these historians so ably describe. The Chinese people, in this view, made a special claim on American concern simply because they were in such comprehensive trouble. Indeed they still are, and the claim is still being made and responded to.

Ironically, Mr. Hunt's chronicle of injustice to the Chinese in America will reinforce the old missionary sentiment of guilt and the need for atonement through good works. History constantly needs revision, yet it slips away slowly. Taiwan and Hong Kong, Reagan and Thatcher, even missionaries and cowboys, are going, going, but hardly gone.

3

Missionary Journalism in China

Missionary history is now coming into its own as a major focus of social history in China. The missionary, by his calling, was the Westerner in closest touch with the Chinese common people; missionary records can therefore tell us something about Chinese life at the popular level.

The American missionaries' response to China's many needs constantly found new forms of expression. The antifootbinding movement and the emancipation of Chinese women from complete male domination, like the missionaries' early support of Chinese nationalistic sentiments against Japan, were examples of this missionary responsiveness. As on the American frontier, when the American forerunner of civilization ran into a problem, he proceeded to attempt a solution. In a China so bogged down in tradition, this attitude was a signal contribution.

• • •

Young J. Allen (1836–1907), a Southern Methodist from Georgia, was the most active of an Anglo-American group of missionaries who published in Chinese the news and comment on the Western world that stimulated the Chinese reform movement of the late nineteenth century. These men, mainly in Shanghai and Peking, worked together in the buoyant faith that Christianity, science, and democratic institutions were integral parts of God's plan for man's material and spiritual progress. Allen in particular saw the emancipation of women as an index of civilized advancement. His edu-

Part of this chapter appeared in the *International Bulletin of Missionary Research,* January 1984, as a review of Adrian A. Bennett, *Missionary Journalist in China: Young J. Allen and His Magazines, 1860–1883* (Athens: University of Georgia Press, 1983).

24

cation at Emory University had given him a grounding in the basic sciences, and while he continued his preaching and promoted schools and a college for Christian nurture, his editing of Chinese periodicals emphasized secular learning, especially science and technology. His *Church News* (*Chiao-hui hsin-pao*) of 1868–1874 he renamed the *Chinese Globe Magazine* (*Wan-kuo kung-pao*) of 1874–1883 and 1889–1907. In 1881–1883 it received a subsidy from the Religious Tract Society, which purchased eight hundred copies (of some two thousand printed) for free distribution to Chinese officials. Because Allen served as superintendent of the Southern Methodist mission in China from 1881 to 1893, he suspended publication in 1883. But he revived the *Wan-kuo kung-pao* in 1889 and continued to put it out until his death in 1907. It became the main focus of his effort. The need for it was evidenced by the publication of half a dozen similar but shorter-lived periodicals in the 1870s and 1880s, in some of which Allen had a hand.

Allen's periodical circulated to all the major centers of East Asia, especially the treaty ports in China. It was the primary vehicle of its kind. It not only spread the Christian message of the missionaries in Chinese but served as an organ of the growing Chinese Christian community, a forum for the presentation of news and views by Chinese Christian writers. These writings are basic materials for the study of the sinicization and institutional growth of Protestant Christianity.

Equally important, Allen's journal spread news of China (including translations or extracts of the *Peking Gazette*) and the international world. The growing preponderance of this type of content led to the change of title in 1874. The result was a pioneer weekly Chinese news magazine (from 1889 to 1907 it was a monthly) with a built-in Christian readership that gradually expanded along with the contents, far beyond the bounds of the Christian religion. The march of late Victorian science and technology, the rise of nationalism and the intensifying of international relations, all made these decades a period of startling news and new developments, which eventually overshadowed the religious subject matter. For a while this journal became a major Chinese window on the world.

Naturally, in this time of growing ferment, the Western editors and Sino-Western contributors sought the regeneration of Chinese life, and seeds of reform were widely sown through this vehicle. Since Chinese historians tend, like cultural patriots in most countries, to filter the foreign sojourner out of the record no matter what his influence, future researchers may expect to find in this journal some traces of Western and native ideas expressed in Chinese that subsequently figured in the reform movement of the 1894–1911 era. Finally, evidences of social change in many forms—for example, the emancipation of Chinese women—appear in these pages.

4

Missionary History as Fiction

Imperialism (or imperial expansion) usually involves some warfare, and this of course commended it to the imperialists by giving them scope for their talent. In comparison with the parade of British overseas heroes, however, Admiral Dewey and General MacArthur are about all we here have to offer from our East Asian annals, even though MacArthur early on had a young staff assistant named Eisenhower. For heroes we Americans have to fall back on our less spectacular institution builders, many of whom were missionaries. Still today we have their impulse to give technology and human rights to China.

John Hersey's The Call *is a pathbreaking book because it makes available to the public a personal account of the missionary experience. Since Hersey is well informed,* The Call *is all the better for being fictional. Missionary memoirs are of course available by the hundreds, but few such works achieve the all-around objectivity that a gifted journalist who came from missionary origins can bring to the task.*

• • •

The Call is an epitaph for 120 years of Protestant missions in China. From 1830 to 1950 the China missions had a steadily growing place in American public sentiment. At the turn of the century John R. Mott of the Student Volunteer Movement for overseas missions called for "the evangelization of the world in this generation," with China as a special target. Unless we can

---

This review of John Hersey's *The Call* (New York: Knopf, 1985) appeared under the title "Mission Impossible" in the *New York Review of Books,* May 30, 1985. Reprinted with permission from the *New York Review of Books.* Copyright © 1985 Nyrev, Inc.

understand the atavism today of Reaganesque piety and Falwellian evangelism, we shall never comprehend how we could have felt so deeply the "loss of China" in the 1950s or initially accepted so casually our crusade to save Vietnam from Communism in the 1960s.

The American opportunity to Christianize China arose from special circumstances. First, the Americans were the only people who came to China by sea for trade and evangelism without thought of territorial aggrandizement. In contrast, the British, the French, the Russians, the Germans, and finally the Japanese all encroached upon China's border regions. Only the Americans, with their New World democracy, felt that they were anti-imperialists. This self-approval, easily perceived by the Chinese, became the basis for the Chinese-American "special relationship." (Scratch our China specialists of today and you will find traces of this in their bloodstreams.)

Our conviction of Sino-American friendship seemed to be confirmed by our privileged status under "extraterritoriality," which meant that a foreign consul had jurisdiction over his nationals in China. This had come from the medieval Chinese practice of letting foreign headmen keep the foreign communities in China, with their strange ways, under control. Eventually Chinese converts to Islam in Central Asia, for example, were allowed to be governed by Islamic law. In the invasion of China by the West after 1842, extraterritoriality became the linchpin of the unequal treaty system. As with other old Chinese customs, the Anglo-Saxons prided themselves on having invented it. The British who ruled India soon after 1860 worked out a division of sovereignty with the Chinese Manchu Ch'ing dynasty that had conquered China. These alien rulers over conquered peoples could understand one another. The result was that missionaries were assimilated into the Chinese ruling class not by mutual love but by Ch'ing imperial policy. They got their chance to attack the outworn evils of Confucianism, the subjection of women, the subordination of youth, from the inside, in the villages. Confucianists rightly saw them as subversive of the old order.

To this circumstance was added the rhythm of Chinese political life, which produced a thirty-eight-year interregnum between the fall of the central government of the Ch'ing dynasty during the

revolution of 1911 and the revival of a central power under Mao
Tse-tung in 1949. During these decades of warlordism, revolution,
and invasion, foreigners had special opportunities to participate
and be helpful or acquisitive in Chinese life. It was a golden age,
the great American experience of semicolonialism. It is a fine thing
if you can get it, as we could, without a sense of guilt for having
set it up. After all, our state of California grew no opium poppies,
as British India did to pay for China's teas and silks.

It is this period of maximum American influence, between 1905
and 1950, that John Hersey deals with in *The Call*. His central
character is David Treadup, a six-foot-four farm boy from upper
New York State, tireless, energetic, and full of good will. During
the forty-five years of his career in China he sees himself as working at the forward edge of the missionary effort. After the comparative failure of evangelism in the nineteenth century and the success of hospitals and schools, David arrives in China in time to
attend the centennial missionary conference of 1907 (one hundred
years after the arrival of the first British Protestant, Robert Morrison, in 1807). The conference is split between the fierce, bewhis-
kered, older evangelists from the back country, who believe in
spreading only the divine word, and the younger newcomers convinced of the need for a social gospel that will meet China's needs
with good works. Treadup is among the latter because he is a YMCA
secretary. In fact when David Treadup is in Tientsin he is put up
by another Y secretary, Roscoe Hersey, whose son, as we can recall
from John Hersey's pieces in the *New Yorker*, was John Hersey.
The Call describes the modern wing of Christian missions, which
was most responsive to Chinese needs and proclivities.

The Protestant denominations reduce the competition among
themselves by agreeing that each will concentrate on certain parts
of China, but they are united in preserving the spirit of the Refor-
mation and in having nothing to do with Roman Catholic missionaries. The early history of the Jesuit mission between the six-
teenth and eighteenth centuries seems barely known to them.
Those who seek to convert upper-class Chinese reformers in the
1890s feel they have devised a new tactic.

Thus Treadup demonstrates his inventiveness by organizing lectures on science to attract the interest of upper-class literati and
officials. Where the Jesuits three hundred years before had used

clocks, prisms, maps, and other products of Western technology, David Treadup lectures on the gyroscope. He holds up a limp chain. Can it be made to climb a ladder at the back of the stage? No? His assistant spins it on a wheel and releases it to roll like a wheel across the stage and up the ladder before losing its momentum. Treadup tours the United States seeking funds from businessmen and collecting equipment with which he sets up a laboratory in Shanghai to produce the machines for his lectures on electricity, aircraft, and other scientific wonders. So successful are these lectures that Treadup goes on tour with James B. Todd (a surrogate for the prominent missionary John R. Mott) to attract audiences for the latter's evangelism; but Treadup's lectures outdraw Todd's by a wide margin. In the China of 1910–1915, as in the late Ming dynasty, science is in, but Christianity still knocks at the door.

The next phase of Treadup's experience is the discovery of the Chinese common man. In the twentieth century the American missionaries in China became increasingly involved in the social problems of a people undergoing a profound transformation. From such a perspective, the evangelism practiced in the United States may have won a few Chinese converts, but to most Chinese it seemed beside the point. David Treadup follows this secular trend when he goes to France along with other YMCA secretaries, including a number of Chinese, to help the Chinese labor corps of some 180,000 men write letters back home. This inspires the Y secretaries to start a literacy movement and helps to stimulate the mass education movement in China. One leader was Y. C. James Yen, known throughout the world as Jimmie Yen, who went into the North China countryside in the 1920s to reach the common people with programs for literacy, public health, and agronomic science. In *The Call*, where Yen appears as "Johnny Wu," Treadup tries to join him, and Wu replies that foreigners are not welcome.

Hersey wants to make the point that the anti-imperialist movement among students during the 1920s, which was inspired by Japan's being left in control of Shantung province in the Versailles peace settlement of 1919, began to concentrate on missionaries as cultural imperialists. Here emerges the intense Chinese patriotism that seeks to dispense with missionary good works because they come from outside the country and seem to support the status quo.

The Call is fascinating to read, partly owing to its organization.

Treadup writes prodigiously, turning out a journal entry or a letter almost every day. When he is interned by the Japanese in 1943, he writes a long, retrospective self-examination called "Search." Hersey is thus able to quote on one page what Treadup wrote at the time, and on the next page what he thought about it forty years later, while Hersey supplies the narrative commentary. The book also gives an authentic sense of the sights, sounds, and smells, the amenities and disasters, of the old China, which have even now not been wholly swept away by modernization. David Treadup is certainly the most articulate writer to have come out of the missionary movement.

Reflecting on his life fifty years later, he attributes his original conversion to missionary work to four factors—personal need, group hysteria, hypnotism by the preacher, and fear for himself. He looks back on the event as a stage in his growing up. When he wants to go to China as a missionary, he finds the mission board require, as was then the custom, that he go as a married man. He is downcast until he discovers that a Miss Emily Kean, whom he had known briefly in college, is still unmarried. They correspond and by mail agree to make a life together. With a wife in prospect, Treadup is fully equipped for the field. He is sent first; she follows but does not marry him until eighteen months later. In his domestic life Treadup holds the missionary's belief that families should be subordinate to the cause. When one of his children dies at the age of two, he is away on one of his frequent excursions.

Of course the missionary life is a very busy one, the missionaries spending much of their time with other missionaries, including the Chinese Christians in the movement. Living in the heat and dirt of Chinese cities and villages, the Treadups relish their vacations at the mountain retreat from the lower Yangtze at Kuling, "a hiding-place from China," or at Peitaiho on the coast north of Tientsin. Here as well they are out of touch with Chinese life. Hersey makes it clear that missionaries on the whole take their culture with them and sedulously maintain it. After all, if they became too Chinese in their habits and outlook, they might lose the missionary impulse.

Still another phase of Treadup's career begins in the 1930s. The home office decides that he has become a mere "humanist," not really devoted to a personal God and His Son as Savior. As Emily says, David is "too full of love for human creatures." He is dropped from the rolls, but manages to get private support for his work and carries on. Soon he has another kind of opportunity. When the Japanese seize Manchuria in 1931 and begin to encroach on North China, the foreign missionaries with their extraterritorial status can be of real help in maintaining their hospitals, colleges, and other good works. They remain immune to Japanese attack until 1941. Caught between Chinese nationalism and Japanese invasion, the missionaries see that their days are obviously numbered, and yet they can continue to be of help.

After Treadup goes into rural work on his own, Hersey gives us a vivid picture of this very tall American visiting his villages on his Indian motorcycle in a cloud of dust and clatter. The crises caused by the local warlords and the Japanese invasion, by famine and disease, crowd his days. These harsh realities eclipse matters of the spirit. When the Japanese finally intern Treadup in 1943, Hersey tells us that he suffers a breakdown of his faith. Emily has been repatriated, he is ill, and his life's work seems to have come to nothing. Neither God nor Jesus seems to be an adequate explanation of the human suffering he has observed.

This loss of faith seems to tell us more about Hersey than about Treadup. The missionary's writings show little concern for spiritual devotion, but a large interest in giving practical help to the Chinese people. He is not the type to collapse under pressure or recant a faith that seems not to have been central to his life in China. I believe John Hersey here is portraying his own disillusionment with the letter of Christianity, a disillusionment he no doubt came to quite early in life. After all, Hersey is himself not a YMCA secretary, but the son of a YMCA secretary. He is using Treadup's loss of faith to represent the passage of Christian evangelism into the dustbin of history, at least in China. The whole panoply of missionary institution-building and helpfulness to the oppressed Chinese people has now had its golden moment and come to an end.

If this is John Hersey's message, he combines it with a full recognition of the American concern for the Chinese people that has been a constant theme in American life. After repatriation by the Japanese, Treadup returns to postwar China to work, first, under the United Nations Relief and Rehabilitation Administration and, later, under the Industrial Cooperative movement. He even gets back to his North China villages until the Communist organizers of 1949 have him vilified in a "struggle meeting" by his peasant friends, who next day greet him warmly on the street. He is expelled from China as a symbol of cultural imperialism and shortly after his return to America dies at the age of seventy-two.

Hersey's labyrinthine account of a great multitude of people and events in modern Chinese history leaves him no time to look at the folklore that spread in America about the China missions. Americanist historians as well have signally failed to examine the subject. They have reached across the Atlantic to our European origins and have followed the westward movement across the continent to the Pacific. But no one has tried to synthesize the lore of the old China trade with that of the new frontier which seemed to open in China in the 1890s. By 1899, in fact, the Open Door became enshrined as the American policy in China. Trade did not notably prosper, but China emerged thereafter as open territory for Christian work.

This American image of China differed profoundly from that of the Russians. Their image of China began with the frightful devastation of southern Russia under the Golden Horde of the Mongols, who erupted westward from China in the thirteenth century. Russia's eastward movement to find a warm-water port on the Pacific had little missionary motive. The Russian Orthodox Church set up an ecclesiastical mission in Peking, but its members ministered only to other Russians and spent their time largely with sinology or alcohol. The Russian march across the Siberian tundra had gained them only an early defeat by the powerful Chinese Ch'ing empire of the Manchus and expulsion in 1689 from the Amur Valley in northern Manchuria. The equivalent American experience of continental expansion had been limited to the conquest of tribal Amerindian chieftains like Sitting Bull and Geronimo, who lacked the abilities of their distant ethnic cousin, the K'ang-hsi emperor of China, victor over the Russians.

Fortunately for us, the Russians never tried to save Chinese souls until the Marxist-Leninist expansion of the Comintern in the 1920s. No doubt the Russian example was central in carrying out China's great revolution, just as Japan's invasion convulsed the Chinese people into a nation. But we can hardly say that the contiguous Russians have had more influence in China than the distant

Americans. When we contemplate our superpower confrontation today, we should recall our anguish when the antichrist of Russian Communism in the 1940s stole China's open door and its Christian potentialities away from us. In the 1980s, when Deng Xiaoping's modernization drive has enlisted our sympathy and support, perhaps we should scrutinize our unconscious motives. Haven't we been here before?

Treadup is an omnicompetent and ubiquitous figure who undertakes practically every sort of activity a missionary might, short of becoming a journalist, a Communist, or a Foreign Service officer (categories that Joe McCarthy soon lumped together). Yet the trend of his life leads him away from religious belief into the world of practical realities. He arranges for the transfer of technology to China and tries to transplant human rights there. Such activities will certainly continue and will make more sense if only we can think about them on the basis of knowledge such as that provided by *The Call*.

5

Sinology Gone Astray:
A Peking Confidence Man

The missionary's chief rival in penetrating the mysteries of Chinese life was the sinologue, who sought entrance through the language and culture. Both types of foreigners naturally gravitated to Peking.

• • •

Peking charmed its Western residents early in this century because it had been a capital city of non-Chinese conquerors and Chinese collaborators for most of a thousand years. Founded in 947 as a capital of the Khitan Mongols' Liao dynasty, it had been used similarly by the Tungusic Chin dynasty between 1122 and 1234, then by the Mongols to 1368, and finally by the Manchus after 1644. When Anglo-French troops marched down its broad avenues in 1860, they were a new phenomenon only in their outlandish appearance. The Chinese servants and tradesmen of the ancient capital accepted the British and other Westerners as they had accepted their predecessors. Soon the Manchu and Chinese bureaucrats had the British helping them to defeat the rebels around Shanghai, just as they had a young Ulsterman, Robert Hart, helping with his Irish sensibility to give them new revenues from the foreign trade. Thus while Britain sought enthusiastically to legitimize, protect, and profit from her commercial expansion, China's rulers made use of British aims and abilities for their own ends within China. The China wing of the British empire was taken *faute de mieux* into the management, incorporated into the Ch'ing dynasty's shaky power structure.

This review of Hugh Trevor-Roper, *Hermit of Peking: The Hidden Life of Sir Edmund Backhouse* (New York: Knopf, 1977), appeared as "The Confidence Man" in the *New York Review of Books*, April 14, 1977. Reprinted with permission from the *New York Review of Books*. Copyright © 1977 Nyrev, Inc.

Foreign residents enjoyed Peking all the more after 1900, when allied Christendom (plus Japan) suppressed the Boxer effort to expel them. The period from 1901 to 1937 (at which point new conquerors came) was a rare and happy time for foreigners in Peking, an era of special perquisites and a special freedom of opportunity, not least to participate in the fringe of Chinese life without being stuck in it. Like Mongol chieftains of the thirteenth century, when Polo saw Cambaluc, or Manchu captains of the seventeenth, when Father Schall headed the astronomical bureau, foreigners in Peking in the early 1900s had an untouchable status (newly known as extraterritoriality) and lived in their own cultural fashion, variously racing their ponies or worshiping their god. To their attentive Chinese servitors in household and office, cultural symbiosis was an old story. Any two Peking Chinese with a deadpan pun could bypass the comprehension of a foreign companion, whose effort to invade their culture through the language, though it showed commendable sincerity, could only put him at their mercy.

On this cultural frontier emerged the China pundit, who interpreted China to the Western public, and the sinologue, whose literacy in Chinese (like that of the Chinese scholar-official class) gave him a distinct and hard-won dignity. The two roles were associated but not easily combined. The China views of G. E. Morrison, the *Times*'s own correspondent, were not inhibited by any knowledge of the language. J. O. P. Bland, who wrote many large popular volumes, had had only the elementary practical Chinese of a Customs apprenticeship. Both these pundits felt the usual need for Chinese documentation and got it at times from the sinologue Edmund Trelawny Backhouse.

In retrospect we can see that Peking must always have produced foreign sinologues who studied Chinese writings and foreign pundits who explained China to their fellow tribesmen. A vigorous pundit like Morrison might even become the obverse of pundit, a foreign adviser who explained the invaders' curious ways to the local Chinese. All these people skated on the thin ice between the two cultures. Sometimes they were seduced by their countrymen's gullible will to believe ("China is a sheet of sand, unorganizable"); for cultural differences are rationally unaccountable and may seem by turns menacing or entrancing (Fu Manchu or Charlie Chan). Only a sinologue of strong character could withstand the temptation to exploit his countrymen's willful credulity concerning "the Chinese." In fact Chinese ways were both sophisticated and secretive. The predictive capacity of China pundits was no greater then than now, and their failures to unscrew the inscrutable often had to be masked by the usual flow of irrelevant circumstantial detail that was the sinologue's stock in trade. The wildest gossip at the Peking Club was simple truth compared with what one could get in Chinese circles in the West City, once one had the entrée.

A well-connected Englishman in Peking between 1901 and 1937 could enjoy maximal freedom to pursue private schemes and fantasies with minimal responsibility for their outcome. Peking was a hothouse forcing bed for romantic role playing. The southeast section of the city outside the armed Legation Quarter was inhabited by remittance men of alcoholic dignity, sociable widows of diplomatic background, superannuated musicians, stranded poets fond of boys, budding art collectors, sincere scholars, patriarchal ex-missionaries, archaeologist-priests, a whole Maughamesque cast of characters, variously motivated but all entranced by the sights, sounds, cuisine, and services of Peking. They were privileged to support servants and dealers, Chinese teachers (mainly Manchu), horse boys, amahs, cooks, guides, ricksha men, cleaning coolies, flower sellers, street peddlers, and many others who could give them contact with Chinese life. The foreign community savored this contact and vied to enjoy it. By the 1930s, however, there was one person whom they knew by name but never saw, the sinologue Sir Edmund Backhouse, baronet, who had left them all behind by going native in the West City.

Hugh Trevor-Roper, Regius Professor of Modern History at Oxford, has exhumed Backhouse's career as one of the great literary forgers. Backhouse's masterpiece was "The Diary of His Excellency Ching-shan," published as a key chapter in *China under the Empress Dowager* (1910), an inside account of late Ch'ing court politics, documented by Backhouse, engagingly written by Bland, and in its time a unique and influential work. This diary Backhouse said he found in Ching-shan's study shortly after his death in 1900 during the post-Boxer looting. Its contents picture the Empress Dowager's confidant and commander, Jung-lu, as a moderate opposed to the Boxer excesses. Scholars have long since exposed its impossibly intelligent anticipations of events and its plagiarism of documents published later, but some—like Bland—clung to the idea that this fabrication had been foisted upon Backhouse, who remained innocent.

Hermit of Peking demolishes this defense once and for all. Sir Edmund turns out to have been a confidence man with few equals, who repeatedly floated great financial schemes in high quarters and with the utmost secrecy, only to have them collapse each time as pure fantasies. Forgery was only one means by which he cleverly launched his dreams upon the world as facts.

Mr. Trevor-Roper's detective work uncovers an impressive sequence of these fakeries. Backhouse's father was a director of Barclay's Bank. A younger brother became Admiral of the Fleet. But Backhouse himself fled Oxford in debt, went through bankruptcy (staying abroad) and turned up in Peking as a remittance man in 1899, aged twenty-five, already a mature imposter. To Sir Robert Hart he brought letters of introduction from the prime minister (Lord Salisbury), the duke of Devonshire, and the colonial secretary (Joseph Chamberlain). This highly connected young man was shy, charming, and gifted at languages, claiming to know several. He soon became a translator of Chinese for Morrison and later for Bland, with whom he eventually collaborated.

Backhouse's forging of the Ching-shan diary was just a beginning. After 1910 he went beyond documentation to a series of enormously exciting practical put-ons. Part of his act was to claim an insider's connections at the top of the other culture, as a close friend of Grand Councilor Wang Wen-shao, Grand Eunuch Li Lien-ying, Viceroy Hsü Shih-ch'ang, Prime Minister Tuan Ch'i-jui, Finance Minister Liang Shih-i, or anyone else appropriate. Such dignitaries were in the same city, often just down the street from the foreigners, but so impenetrable was the cultural-linguistic-social gap that few foreigners could ever question them about their friendship with Backhouse. He had the transcultural field to himself.

In 1910 he wangled a contract to be the agent of the great shipbuilding firm John Brown & Co. By 1916 his "negotiations" with the Chinese government led the firm to produce "estimates and designs for six coastal-defence vessels of 10,400 tons for the Chinese navy." But just then Backhouse disappeared from Peking and the deal evaporated.

Meantime he had pursued his great Chinese arms caper: in

1915, he became a secret agent for the British minister Sir John Jordan, to purchase arms privately in China for use in Europe against Germany. The demand came from the War Office and Lord Kitchener himself. Backhouse, being so well connected in both Britain and China, seemed the logical choice to take sole charge of this delicate matter (China was neutral, Germany could object). Soon he reported success in locating hundreds of thousands of Mauser and Mannlicher rifles, hundreds of Krupp machine guns and field guns, all stashed away by local generals. He negotiated busily far and wide. Arms were "shipped" down the Yangtze. Deal followed deal. Money came from England. Vessels with arms left Shanghai for Hong Kong. Sir Edward Grey at the Foreign Office offered to ask Japan to send a cruiser to convoy them. The ships stopped at Foochow, but were rerouted and delayed at Canton.

Jordan, at the height of his career as the most powerful and knowledgeable diplomat in China, finally went directly to President Yuan Shih-k'ai to get action, but Yuan inscrutably "professed complete ignorance of the whole transaction." So circumstantially had Backhouse built up his fantasy in secret reports and cipher cables, including even German "diplomatic protests" to Yuan, that it took some time for the Foreign Office to become unmesmerized. Jordan had Backhouse tell the whole story to the top government fixer-financier, Liang Shih-i, who was amazed and said he thought Backhouse had been duped. Jordan reported "there has evidently been a split between Liang and the party with which Backhouse was working." So strong was Backhouse's plausibility! Only by degrees did Jordan conclude that it had all been a hoax, fortunately a secret one.

Meanwhile the fecund Backhouse had started on his great banknote scheme. He "negotiated" a secret deal for the American Bank Note Company to be "the sole foreign printers of Chinese money for ten years." The amount to be printed escalated. After Backhouse had had four personal "interviews" with President Yuan, the amount was to be 650 million banknotes. Late in 1916 Backhouse came to New York to report in person to the company. Back in Peking he handed over the Chinese contracts signed by president and prime minister. He received £5,600 commission. Then nothing happened. Finally the company's agent went to court, Backhouse holed up in British Columbia, and his family bailed him out.

Since all these episodes had been kept secret, together with a number of similar incidents over the years, Backhouse had been able to nurture an academic career simultaneously. In 1913 he presented to the Bodleian Library a genuinely valuable collection of Chinese books including, for example, half a dozen volumes of the rare Yung-lo encyclopedia of the early 1400s. The seventeen thousand items in this collection were a real treasure. Oxford thanked him officially. He was elected to fill the chair of Chinese at King's College, London. His second volume with Bland, *Annals and Memoirs of the Court of Peking* (1914), was published and acclaimed.

But he pulled back from this career, pleading illness and eye trouble. After the war began, he resigned the King's College chair and returned to Peking. Later gifts to the Bodleian eventually became make-believe, winding up as the "famous Palace Library" in fifty-eight thousand volumes, which had to be transported seven hundred miles by cart to a railhead in West Kansu before being shipped from Tientsin. The Bodleian never recovered the funds it had advanced.

The final and conclusive proof of fakery, if any is needed, was provided by Sir Edmund himself in the two volumes of scabrous memoirs he wrote for the Swiss representative in Peking, shortly before his death there in January 1944. They again offer detailed inventions to support the authenticity of the Ching-shan diary, but are at the same time an obsessively pornographic, homosexual account of a lifetime's copulation with a long succession of the great figures of the age, including Prime Minister Lord Rosebery ("a slow and protracted copulation which gave equal pleasure to both parties") and also sexual services to the Empress Dowager, whom Backhouse estimates he saw for this purpose between one hundred fifty and two hundred times! Yet even when fantasy ran wild, circumstantial details accompanied it.

Hermit of Peking is a fascinating book, not only for its bizarre revelations but also because it is constructed like a detective story. Mr. Trevor-Roper is a deft narrator; he takes the reader along with him, and stranger events lie always around the corner. In the end he judges Backhouse's personality with all its fantasies as "complete, coherent and sane." The success in beguiling others came from "personal charm . . . transparent honesty . . . apparent realism . . . practical toughness" and the "extraordinary circumstantiality" and "minute and scrupulous detail" of his concoctions, together with methods of operation that required a patron, enjoined secrecy, and left him the only reporter of his doings.

As to motivation, we can only speculate. Mr. Trevor-Roper sees Backhouse as a snob, rebelling against a Quaker middle-class background, led on by "the 'aestheticism,' the febrile eroticism, the aggressive, insolent deviation of the 1890s." With this "empty" and "supercilious elitism" he turned against his own origins and escaped to China, eventually winding up in the direction of fascism. Professor Jonathan Spence's review of the English edition, *A Hidden Life (Times Literary Supplement,* October 29, 1976), offers further evidence of possible motivation, including an unnoticed baby brother, born a year later than Edmund, who died at the age of three and was commemorated in the names of the twin boys that were born next, the favored and successful ones. In the opening paragraphs above I have tried to suggest how the Peking milieu could have fostered a young bounder's proclivities—being bilingual could quickly lead him into a culturally ambiguous double life.

The Backhouse story will keep on growing in interest. Mr. Spence comments on the light that Backhouse's schemes cast on Western imperialism—the naiveté, ignorance, and "casual stupidity" of national governments and business corporations. *Hermit of Peking* opens doors into many questions. The Chinese side is plainly still underresearched. As Trevor-Roper notes, the liberties Backhouse took with documents in *Annals and Memoirs* moved Kenneth Scott Latourette to critical comments in his survey, *The Chinese.* Bland's threat of a libel suit led Macmillan, in Latourette's absence, to insert "an apologetic erratum slip." (One is reminded of the same firm's suppression of Ross Koen's *China Lobby* after printing it in the 1950s.) The whole Bland and Backhouse contribution to history needs critical reappraisal and a new synthesis.

Sinology is of course the natural habitat of nitpickers. A personage called "Mr. Yu Chuan-pu" sounds suspiciously like "Mr. Ministry of Posts and Communications," evidently a garble by Lord ffrench. Again, though the Ching-shan diary was said to be "in a very difficult 'grass-hand,'" the part of it shown in facsimile is more like the easier correspondence style (*hsing-shu*, not *ts'ao-tzu*). To what extent was Backhouse, even in his memoirs, simply drawing on the extensive Chinese scatological literature on the late Ch'ing court? To what extent on live informants? Had he had any contact with Jung-lu's family?

While Mr. Trevor-Roper has described his sources rather fully in general terms and supplies a list of some seventy-five "source notes" for various pages, his account mercifully is not footnoted in Ph.D. style, and avid readers will no doubt be after him for further guidance. A whole Backhouse industry may develop. In fact, controversy has already started.

Mr. Trevor-Roper got onto the Backhouse story when he was given the two volumes of memoirs at Basel airport in 1973 to examine and deposit in the Bodleian. The Swiss representative who had befriended Backhouse in wartime and commissioned him to do his memoirs was Dr. Reinhard Hoeppli, who had been a leading parasitologist at the Peking Union Medical College in the 1930s. (My wife, Wilma, edited some articles for him there in 1933.) Before his death in 1973 he had prepared the memoirs for publication and had written a postscript of his own to appraise their value and record his contact with the author. In six issues of the *TLS* (November to January), Mr. Richard Ellmann of New College has written thrice "in defence of Dr. Hoeppli" and has been answered thrice by Mr. Trevor-Roper of Oriel, on the issue of how far Hoeppli was taken in by Backhouse (he was). Both writers cite Hoeppli's postscript in the Bodleian, which is unavailable to their readers, and mince no words. This kind of exchange is evidently the modern substitute for a duel. If words could wound, both would be in hospital, Mr. Ellmann on the danger list. There is every indication that Sir Edmund will live in history.

6

Two Faces of Japanese Imperialism in China

The news that Mr. Reagan's "peacekeeper" in Japanese waters is to be a better-armed Japan makes one think back to the half-century of Japan's military expansion from 1894 to 1945. Fortunately a nation that has beaten its swords into Toyotas seems unlikely to revert to militarism as a way of life. But the springs of Japan's modern performance, whether military or industrial, must have a message for us. How an island people poor in natural resources came from behind and have now almost got ahead of us in material technology seems worth pondering. The answer plainly lies in the immaterial realm of motivation.

Two autobiographical accounts from different kinds of leaders—a cabinet minister and a conspirator in revolution—illustrate that drive. Both were written in self-defense by public figures who were under attack at the time. Count Mutsu was foreign minister during the Sino-Japanese war of 1894–1895. Miyazaki Toten was the most prominent Japanese supporter of Sun Yat-sen around the turn of the century. Mutsu and Miyazaki shared the Japanese sense of mission to superintend the westernization of the rest of East Asia. In the 1890s, as forty years of transformation under Western contact brought Japan onto the world stage as a great power, its

This review of Mutsu Munemitsu, *Kenkenroku: A Diplomatic Record of the Sino-Japanese War, 1894–1895,* ed. and trans. Gordon Mark Berger (Princeton: Princeton University Press, 1982; Tokyo: University of Tokyo Press, 1982), and of Miyazaki Toten, *My Thirty-Three Years' Dream: The Autobiography of Miyazaki Toten,* trans. Marius B. Jansen and Etō Shinkichi (Princeton: Princeton University Press, 1982), appeared as "The Real Stuff" in the *New York Review of Books,* April 14, 1983. Reprinted with permission from the *New York Review of Books.* Copyright © 1983 Nyrev, Inc.

sense of mission was still pristine and unsullied. Its future seemed full of promise and possibilities. One chief hope was to regenerate China, and indeed the Chinese revolution that brought Sun Yat-sen to prominence in 1911 was largely made in Japan—partly inspired by its example, partly supported by Japan's pan-Asianist "men of high purpose," latter-day *ronin* looking for an adventurous cause on the mainland.

Miyazaki Toten (1870–1922) was a big, bearded fierce-looking man, full of high-sounding sentiments and loudly dedicated to a great altruistic cause if he could only find it while sober. His self-image as a "man of high purpose" was a vestige of Japanese feudalism in decay, when masterless samurai still aspired to be purely dedicated. They knew their martial arts and held themselves above the honest labor of commoners, but had trouble finding a useful place in society. Their Western counterpart, if they had one, would be somewhere between a knight-errant and a Hollywood private eye.

Miyazaki's *Thirty-Three Years' Dream* was published in installments in 1902, when he was thirty-three by Japanese count, and after he had scandalously bungled the shipment of arms to Sun Yat-sen's revolt in 1900 at Waichow near Hong Kong. One surmises that the author's strategy to clear himself of the suspicion of corruption was to tell all and so make it plain that his entire life had been a well-intentioned bungle and that he was simply incapable of planned corruption, let alone planned revolution. At any rate, Toten's ruthlessly frank and very engaging autobiography reveals him as romantic and generous of spirit but in daily life a sake-swilling whore chaser, sentimentally devoted to his vague cause of rebellion as well as to his fellow conspirators and drinking companions and to his prostitute-friend of the moment (his little black book listed 285 of them). He was given to grand gestures and impulsive bravado rather than to practicality, the kind of man who could embark most urgently for Hong Kong only to find next day that the ship would stop at five places during eighteen days en route. With Miyazaki Toten as his trusted supporter, Sun Yat-sen truly had little need of enemies to thwart his plans. Twenty-two years would pass and Toten would be dead before Sun Yat-sen would finally find Comintern and Soviet helpers whose arms would actually arrive on time.

The exemplary trans-Pacific collaboration of Professors Jansen and Etō has now given us a well-annotated translation of Toten's famous and popular book. Their introduction gives Toten his due as an idealist of courage—chivalrous and unselfish. Though a rebel by nature, Toten was paid for a time as an agent of the Japanese government. He tried to secure unity and cooperation among the leaders of the Chinese secret societies. In 1898 he escorted the ousted reformer K'ang Yu-wei from Hong Kong to Japan and tried to bring K'ang and Sun Yat-sen together so as to unify the Chinese revolutionaries. All in vain.

Behind all this derring-do, the human appeal of Toten's book lies partly in its vivid adventures and partly in its shrewd depiction of romantic ideals frustrated by personal foibles. Toten left his mother, wife, and children in dire poverty and he himself lived on handouts. He spent much of the time in a dream world. "I imagined myself entering the Chinese continent in front of a host of Chinese, a general mounted on a white horse . . . I would cry for joy and fortify myself with sake. At other times . . . the white-robed general would fall victim to the enemy assassin's dagger . . . I would end up heading for the geisha house . . . That white-robed general [was] . . . but a phantom of my high ambition . . . I hadn't come to realize that half my life was made up of sake and sex . . . How could I square such behavior with my original resolve to restore humanity?"

Count Mutsu Munemitsu (1844–1897) had no such problem. In fact, he had tuberculosis and died of it within two years of completing his service as foreign minister. He came from the minor feudal domain of Tosa, and his translator, Gordon Mark Berger, suggests that this gave him both the incentive to participate in the Meiji regime dominated by men from the great fiefs of Satsuma and Choshu and the capacity to view their oligarchy with the objectivity of an outsider. He joined their new government, but "in 1878 he was implicated in a Tosa-centered plot to overthrow the regime" and as a result spent five years in prison. However, the oligarchy then took him onto their team—partly for his ability, partly to placate the popular rights movement with which Mutsu had been associated. He served for two years as Japan's minister to Washington, then in 1892 became foreign minister in Itō Hiro-bumi's first cabinet under the new constitution.

Mutsu's realpolitik in 1894 and 1895 accomplished far more than Miyazaki Toten ever dreamed of. In a little over twelve months Japan became dominant in Korea; spectacularly defeated the Chinese army and navy, contrary to general expectations; and at the same time freed Japan of the unequal treaty system (which gave special advantages to Western nations and continued to impair China's sovereignty for another half-century). Meanwhile Mutsu parried a succession of efforts by the Western powers to intervene and so forestall a complete upset of East Asian power relations. In the peace terms extorted at Shimonoseki from the Chinese leader Li Hung-chang, Japan secured both Taiwan and the Liaotung peninsula of southern Manchuria. Within a few days a triple intervention by the Russians, French, and Germans demanded that Liaotung be given back to China, and Japan complied. Yet the Japanese empire had been born. The Anglo-Japanese alliance followed in 1902 (until 1922), and Japan defeated Russia in Manchuria in 1905. The rising sun shone over East Asia.

Mutsu was at the center of these achievements, mounting a diplomatic offensive through able ministers in London, St. Petersburg, and other capitals. Step by step he worked with Prime Minister Itō, persuaded the cabinet oligarchs, and made use of a vociferous jingoism among the Japanese public. He combined force and guile in Korea, browbeat the Chinese, and all the time showed a punctilious concern for the niceties of international law and the special interests of the Western powers. He and his ministers abroad had to negotiate the new, equal treaties in the midst of a war that threatened the great powers' interests. He had to get the Shimonoseki Treaty of April 17, 1895, ratified in spite of the Triple Intervention that undid part of it on April 23. (Japan accepted the Triple Intervention on May 4, exchanged ratifications of the Sino-Japanese peace treaty on May 8, and gave back Liaotung to China by an imperial rescript on May 10.) Such diplomatic footwork has seldom been equaled. Eliza never crossed such thin and treacherous ice.

Once all this was accomplished, Mutsu collapsed and was replaced as foreign minister by Saionji on June 5, 1895. Japanese jingoists, drunk with glory, and opposition politicos, seeing a good chance, stridently attacked the return of Liaotung to the Chinese, and Mutsu in self-defense wrote a documented inside account of the year's work. *Kenkenroku,* as he called it, cut too close to the bone of truth, however. Prime Minister Ito found it "disquieting," and it was kept from being published until 1929.

Mr. Berger's translation and notes seem to be models of their kind except for one matter of editorial policy. The title *Kenkenroku* will of course be meaningful to those familiar with the Japanese pronunciation of obscure Chinese phrases in the *Classic of Changes.* Others may be told that it means "a record of strenuous effort." Its eye-catching quality nevertheless raises the question whether the Princeton University Press prefers esoteric chic to intelligibility. In this spirit the bibliography and notes cite many Japanese, Korean, and Chinese writings but only in romanization and without characters. Surely a layman intelligent enough to read this well-made book deserves to have English translations added to such titles. She or he might have an amateur interest in the sources being used.

As Mutsu sets forth the rationale of policy at each stage of Japan's aggression, it becomes plain that he would have had a lot in common with John Foster Dulles and his brother Allen. At first, the reason for sending troops to Korea in 1894 was to maintain a balance of power there with China. "We were determined to have the Chinese be the aggressors." But when both Chinese and Japanese forces had arrived there, "in the absence of . . . even a plausible pretext for hostilities, no *casus belli* existed . . . it now became essential to devise some sort of diplomatic strategy paving the way for a transformation of this state of affairs." The result was the Japanese demand for reform of the antiquated Korean government, a reform that a still-antiquated China could hardly accept. The Chinese cleverly replied that "Japan clearly had no right to intervene because she had recognized Korea's independence." This stubborn attempt "to restrict the scope of our rights," Mutsu wrote, showed how the Chinese "were prisoners of their own arrogance."

The Japanese seized the Korean king, who installed in power the aged Taewon'gun, a sort of Confucian ayatollah who execrated all modernity. Mutsu candidly goes on to explain why reform in Korea then proved impossible, thus vitiating Japan's reason for being there. As a hard-nosed realist he "saw no need whatsoever to launch any crusades in the name of national chivalry . . . I had never felt that Korea's internal reform was very important in itself." It was simply a convenient pretext. One begins to understand why *Kenkenroku* was kept under wraps for thirty-four years.

A poignant moment occurred when Itō and Mutsu at Shimonoseki forced their peace terms on Li Hung-chang, whose army and navy they had just destroyed. By refusing to grant a cease-fire they had the old man (Li was seventy-two) in a vise—either accept Japan's terms at once or see the war come ever closer to Peking. But four days after beginning negotiations on March 20, Li was shot in the eye by a would-be Japanese assassin. Suddenly all Japan was deeply humiliated by this treatment of a guest. The empress herself prepared bandages. Itō and Mutsu feared that if Li went home ill, foreign powers might at last intervene and Japan would lose control of the situation. They finally persuaded the cabinet to agree to a cease-fire, and Li continued to negotiate, swathed in bandages in his bedroom. By the time the Triple Intervention did occur, Itō and Mutsu were able to handle it.

During the strenuous spring of 1895 the emperor was in residence, and the cabinet and even the new Diet held meetings at Hiroshima, just fifty years before its destruction. By that later date both the realistic skill of Mutsu and the romantic adventurism of Miyazaki Toten had long since been inherited by Japan's imperial expansionists. As we confront today the rise of Sony, Mitsubishi, Nissan, and other Japanese participants in American life, perhaps we can see some of the same sterling qualities at work in a more constructive mode.

7

Joe Stilwell, All-American, and His Mission to China

Stilwell and MacArthur were the two American theater command-
ers in the war against Japan. Both were West Pointers of outstand-
ing ability, but their careers in World War II could not be less sim-
ilar. MacArthur was aided by the United States Navy, which was
making the Pacific into an American lake. He was also returning
to a former American colony, where he was already enshrined in
history. Stilwell, in contrast had a theater called China-Burma-
India, which stretched across the mountains of North Burma going
quite against nature. China and India had had little communica-
tion across this area. It had its own savage tribesmen, its rivers
flowing south to make trouble for east-west communication. Nei-
ther China nor India was a focus of great strategic importance after
1942. Whacking his way through the jungle in this little-known
area, far from the limelight, Joe Stilwell showed enormous de-
termination, but little of importance came of his effort. While
MacArthur went on to rule Japan, Stilwell died at the end of
the war.

•   •   •

Joe Stilwell had all the best American traits of character—energy,
ingenuity, grit, gumption, self-deprecation. You quickly identify
with him. These are the same virtues that have taken us onto the
moon, into Vietnam and Cambodia, and over Laos. In short, Stilwell is a paragon of those all-American virtues that are leading us
to our compound disaster at home and abroad. This moral sug-

This chapter is a condensation and revision of reviews that originally appeared
in the *New Republic*, March 27, 1971, and in *Business Week*, February 13, 1971,
of Barbara W. Tuchman, *Stilwell and the American Experience in China, 1911–
45* (New York: Macmillan, 1971).

gests itself forcibly in our current mood of reappraisal. Stilwell was about the best we had to offer to meet China's wartime problems, but what he had to offer was not good enough. He couldn't scratch where it itched. The American effort in China in World War II was not geared in with the Chinese Revolution. It was largely irrelevant to the needs of the people.

Stilwell was an intelligent and hard-driving young West Pointer who trained himself to meet the demands of duty, honor, country. He had already made himself an athlete, both a quarterback and a quarter-miler at Yonkers High in New York. At West Point he survived the hazing of plebe year (though a couple of boys unfortunately died) and continued to be an athlete despite his medium stature and slight build. He was a born competitor. By 1904 he was with the infantry in the Philippines; by 1906 he was back at West Point instructing in French and Spanish and coaching athletics (he had introduced basketball). In the summers he got assignments to travel in Guatemala and Mexico, and then in 1911 to the Philippines again by way of Japan and China, where at the end of the year he took a first look at the Chinese Revolution. He had already acquired his special interest in foreign peoples and languages on the American frontier in the Far East.

After teaching again at West Point (this time history and Spanish), Stilwell, like all his military generation, was suddenly yanked out of the peripheral routines of the peacetime army by America's entry into World War I. In 1917 he was thirty-four and ready to prove himself. First he found that he had a special knack as a trainer of troops. The American army's task, as at Plattsburgh, was to train a million men in no time flat. But soon Major Stilwell was needed in France to talk French with our allies. He became a G-2 planner of the Saint-Mihiel offensive, where he worked with George C. Marshall as G-3, head of operations. Saint-Mihiel was a success, and talented soldiers made their mark for the future before peace supervened and the army shrank back to its peacetime size. The military was not yet a major industry.

In 1919 Stilwell escaped the peacetime doldrums by becoming the first army language officer appointed to China. He began with Chinese language study at Berkeley and then went to Peking. Much of the 1920s he spent in North China, first as a language student under the legation for three years and then, for another three years, with the Fifteenth Infantry at Tientsin, where George Marshall had preceded him. Finally, Stilwell spent the late 1930s as military attaché at Peking. During these assignments he traveled all over the country. He acquired a great fondness for the common people and for the rugged outdoor life that travel in China required.

The charm of China for the American in the 1930s came not merely from his special privileges as a foreigner under the unequal treaties, or his superior modernity, education, and technology. The real charm came from the Chinese people themselves, so burdened with human problems, so steadfast in their capacity to make the best of them. By the time of Pearl Harbor, Stilwell was by all odds the top military specialist on the Chinese scene, intimately acquainted with wide stretches of terrain and with the leading personalities and their overwhelming problems.

When Marshall was jumped to become chief of staff in the crisis of 1941, Stilwell was the best American military man for China purposes; but between his assignments overseas, Stilwell's performance in the United States had singled him out also as one of the best leaders of troops in the professional army. During peacetime the army had of course dwindled almost out of sight again, and in September 1939 it numbered only 174,000 men. In maneuvers Stilwell showed uncommon initiative and ingenuity, a real aptitude for blitzkrieg. By 1940 he was a general in command of a division in training in California. He was not "book-bound" but inventive, absolutely unsparing of himself and others, and "very cold-blooded" about people's performance. He kept in close touch with his men and was already well known for his hostility to anyone who put on airs. He led marches himself, wore informal dress, and loved to talk with GIs.

Shortly after Pearl Harbor, Stilwell was picked by Marshall to command GYMNAST, which was to be the first American offensive of the war in North Africa. From the evidence of maneuvers Marshall considered him "a masterly tactician, fertile, ingenious, and confident; a student of military history and excellent in training." Stilwell was the first among the Army's nine corps commanders in order of merit, and if he had eventually commanded the North African landing, no doubt he would have gone on up in the European theater, at least to a post comparable to Bradley's. But the Chinese crisis changed all that.

The epic struggle between Stilwell and Chiang Kai-shek can be viewed in several frameworks, from several angles. These two men were not merely strong personalities but exemplars of leading traits in their two countries. From the point of view of the Chinese Revolution, Stilwell's criticisms of the miserable evils in the Chinese military establishment contribute to our understanding of the Kuomintang collapse. Chiang had an outworn power structure based on loyalty, not efficiency. Stilwell sympathized with the common soldier and distrusted Chinese officers in general because of their corruption and callousness.

Stilwell's effort to reform and build up a modern Chinese army would sooner or later have dissolved the old military power structure on top of which Chiang Kai-shek performed his central balancing act. The starving conscripts, officer corruption, hoarded supplies, and loyalty-before-merit of the Nationalist forces, added to the stress and exhaustion of resisting Japan, fostered a strongly conservative status quo.

Our World War II China policy was one of using fair words, money, and military supplies to keep Chinese fighting Japanese on our behalf. But it was also a naive FDR concept that postwar China could somehow be aided to fill the power vacuum left by the defeat of Japan—an American idea that never came off, since it overlooked the fact of the Chinese Revolution.

If Stilwell's remaking of the Chinese army had been allowed to proceed, it would have created troops and commanders who would eventually have shattered Chiang's power structure and no doubt produced some kind of military takeover. Chiang could see it coming. In dealing with Stilwell, Chiang was up against a hard-bitten efficiency expert with a fanatical drive for combat achievement, backed by the influence of American supplies, whereas neither efficiency nor combat was Chiang's major concern. He was against the revolution that the Communists had long since captured out from under him, and the Chinese war effort demanded by the Americans could only be further unsettling to the status quo. The tendency would be to get the Chinese Communists into it with American supplies, but this would quite upset Chiang's rickety applecart. He had to fight off Stilwell's being given real command. Chiang succeeded in blocking this attempt and in getting Stilwell recalled in October 1944.

After his repeated efforts to mount an offensive against the Japanese and for that purpose to create a modern Chinese army in India, Stilwell finally discovered that in the last analysis the generalissimo did not want a modernized force of such proportions—because of the danger that he could not himself control it. Furthermore, Nationalist China was exhausted, and the tendency in Chungking to sit out the latter part of the war (Pearl Harbor was hailed as "Armistice Day" in China) can readily be understood against this background.

Stilwell's efforts were further complicated by Chiang's traditionalist theories of strategy and tactics. Following the ancient classic on warfare, the *Sun-tzu,* he stressed the value of the defensive posture, of letting the enemy move first and then trapping him, of never offering battle except with a great superiority of forces.

In this situation nothing could have been less appropriate than Stilwell's energetic determination first to meet the Japanese head on in Burma and then, when driven out, to fight his way back. China was simply not a country ready for any more war. North Burma, with its jungle-filled valleys running southward, was terrible terrain to cross from east to west with a road and pipeline. Stilwell's achievement in driving his campaign across Burma and back to China was therefore an epic of high quality. Here was one of our most dynamic commanders shunted to a forlorn assignment at the most distant end of a supply line that had the lowest priority. Added to all this was the unexpected technological feat by which the navy and air force finally reduced Japan across the Pacific and made a base in China unnecessary. By the time Stilwell reached his showdown with Chiang over the American demand that he be given command of the Chinese forces, the war effort in China was beginning to lose its value against Japan. American aid now figured mainly in China's domestic politics.

If we seek a perspective on Stilwell from the point of view of the American expansion abroad, the story comes out somewhat differently. Stilwell lost out but so did Chiang. First of all, the Americans, with an overriding self-righteousness, were bent on killing Japs to win the war; it was the mission for which the military had been trained, which formed their ethos. In pursuit of this goal the American military were the slaves of technological progress, obliged by their sense of duty to develop quickly all the potentialities of organization and firepower and get results in combat. The American military mission was not primarily, nor even secondarily, political. Where the *Sun-tzu* had set the aim of warfare as bending the opponent to one's will and getting him to surrender by whatever means, the American military technicians were more concerned with creating striking forces and solving the problems of logistics and supplies necessary to lay down a field of fire. What might happen after peace broke out was distinctly not their responsibility. They were trained not to think about it.

Added to this difference in style and aim was the fact that the Americans were using China for the allegedly common purpose of defeating Japan. They complained when China did not want to be so used and seemed more concerned with its domestic revolution. At this point the Americans, as foreigners, could do little to affect the Chinese situation. Stilwell got some of his Chinese-speaking State Department officers up to see the Communists at Yenan, and this Military Observer Mission (naturally named the "Dixie Mission" because it was a mission to the rebels) momentarily opened up the chance that the Americans and the Chinese Communists might develop a working relationship and at least avoid fighting each other. This constructive possibility was quickly torpedoed, however, by the gut reactions and general mindlessness of our ambassador (Hurley) in a situation where American power, demonstrated in the coming victory over Japan, seemed to make objectivity and the weighing of realities in China unnecessary.

Although no one has wanted to spell it out, the idea of an American general really commanding Chinese armies in the protorevolutionary China of the 1940s was a prescription full of poison. It could very well have got the American military lined up in the name of law and order against the revolution. It was of a piece with the naive American assumption that Chiang's *ancien régime* could somehow be saved by "reform." Stilwell's command of China's forces might have eventuated in a far greater disaster than his recall. His candidacy showed the bankruptcy of our attempt to mastermind a war effort from an exhausted regime.

Stilwell is thus enshrined for us as a symbol of American know-how and fortitude, the can-do spirit, dynamic and indomitable, a curmudgeon but a humane and efficient one. He lived his China career in the time of Sino-American friendship, when we had a good deal of contact people to people. Happily for him, he did not live to see us become enemies, and he did not enter the nuclear age of limited wars, when the old all-out virtues not only cannot ensure our survival but actually endanger it. Stilwell is on the roll of great captains, from Hannibal to Robert E. Lee, who tried and were foiled by fate. They all seem to have lived a long time ago, in a past age when heroism was sufficient unto itself.

8

Douglas MacArthur and American Militarism

Dugout Doug, as some GIs called him, was actually brave beyond belief, courting death hundreds of times to set his troops an example. He was in fact our greatest soldier, a field general in three wars over a third of a century (1918–1951), who commanded more troops in battle with fewer casualties than any other American. He also got into more public controversy. His vanity constantly showed through, and when it came to politics, people sensed that he had no social or economic program to substitute for victory. His performances in war and as a latter-day shogun in Japan made history, but that is essentially what they were—performances.

Yet the exploits in MacArthur's career are so various—"noble and ignoble, inspiring and outrageous, arrogant and shy, . . . protean, . . . ridiculous, . . . sublime," as Manchester writes—that each event leads back to the question of personality: What self-image motivated MacArthur? What did he think he was doing?

The bits and pieces for an understanding can be found in Manchester's *American Caesar*, a psychic Erector Set. The girders, nuts, and bolts are all laid out, inviting us to put together our own model of the general's remarkable personality.

The initial element is the hero father. In November 1863, when eighteen thousand Union troops, exceeding orders, stormed the heights of Missionary Ridge above Chattanooga, Captain Arthur MacArthur of the Twenty-fourth Wisconsin planted the first flag

This review of William Manchester, *American Caesar: Douglas MacArthur, 1880–1964* (Boston: Little, Brown, 1978), appeared as "Digging out Doug" in the *New York Review of Books*, October 12, 1978. Reprinted with permission from the *New York Review of Books*. Copyright © 1978 Nyrev, Inc.

on the summit. He showed himself absolutely fearless in a dozen other battles, and at age nineteen became the youngest colonel in the United States Army. After that, however, army life was reduced to Indian wars or military politics in Washington, and Arthur MacArthur was made brigadier general only when sent to Manila in 1898. In charge of catching Aguinaldo and suppressing the Philippine Republic, he was already creating the MacArthur style—that of a smart professional soldier and imaginative field commander, fearless in exposing himself to enemy fire, considerate of his troops, generous in rewarding subordinates (who included Peyton March and John J. Pershing), given to global pronouncements with a prosy grandiloquence ("ethnological homogeneity," wrote Arthur MacArthur, "induces men to respond . . . to the appeals of consanguineous leadership"), intolerant of civilian interference, eager for praise, convinced that Washington was against him, and inclined to censor journalists' dispatches.

According to his aide, "Arthur MacArthur was the most flamboyantly egotistical man I had ever seen, until I met his son." Unable to work in tandem at Manila with William Howard Taft, he was ordered home in 1901; but "he simply could not refrain from speaking out of turn," criticizing the War Department or the White House or prophesying war with Japan or Germany. Lieutenant General MacArthur, although the army's senior general, was passed over for chief of staff, and at sixty-four he resigned his commission, bitterly disappointed. His son Douglas followed in his footsteps but went farther in every direction.

The second influence was a determined mother, a southern belle from Norfolk, who nightly told little Douglas, "You must grow up to be a great man like your father" (or alternatively "like Robert E. Lee"). She dressed him in skirts "and kept his hair in long curls until he was eight." But at West Texas Military Academy he made himself shortstop and quarterback, top scholar and valedictorian. For a competitive examination to get his West Point nomination, his mother got him a special tutor. He scored 99⅓ percent. During his four years at West Point she lived just off the plain at Craney's Hotel, and he usually saw her daily before dinner.

These parental compulsions were visited upon a young man of great innate ability and personal charm, whose first recollections were of bugles and riding boots at forts on the Wild West frontier and whose whole life aimed at military leadership. At West Point he wound up as first captain of the corps, like Robert E. Lee and John J. Pershing. Wars were conveniently spaced to give him opportunity. His exploits were amazing—at forward reconnaissance, for instance. In France MacArthur not only led his men over the top, at night he crawled through battlefields to appraise the results. The night after the American victory at Saint-Mihiel, he and his adjutant crept through no-man's-land and through the German lines, and from a hilltop observed the enemy's disorder. He reported that an attack could make a breakthrough; but headquarters had its own preconceptions and the chance was lost. In France MacArthur received seven Silver Stars for bravery.

His personal getup was already distinctive and contrary to regulations—a four-foot muffler, a turtleneck sweater, no helmet, no gas mask, a riding crop but no arms. This visibility and his frontline courage were part of his charisma as a leader of men. But he also mastered his planning and paperwork, never forgot anything, and trained his staff to handle their specialties while he was with his troops.

The seamier record—servile letters toadying to superiors with heavy-handed flattery—show another MacArthur. For example, there is a letter from his mother to Pershing soliciting her son's promotion to brigadier general: "A little heart-to-heart letter emboldened by the thought of my late husband's great admiration for you . . . I know the Secretary of War and his family quite intimately, and the Secretary is very deeply attached to Colonel MacArthur and knows him quite well . . . I am told by the best authority that if my son's name is on your list . . . he will get the promotion."

He made brigadier general in 1918. Later, after becoming a major general in 1925, he wanted to be chief of staff, and in 1930 he wrote the secretary of war, Patrick J. Hurley, that Hurley's routine report on the Philippines was "the most statesmanlike utterance that has emanated from the American Government in many decades . . . a great and courageous piece of work, and I am sure that the United States intends even greater things for you in the future." Hurley of course agreed.

In 1932 MacArthur's public image looked its worst as Hoover's chief of staff when he used tanks, gas, bayonets, and brutality to disperse the unarmed crowd of twenty-five thousand veterans, some with families, who had converged on Washington as "bonus marchers" seeking relief. (Their pitiful story is in William Manchester's *The Glory and the Dream: A Narrative History of America 1932–1972*.) His assistant, Major Eisenhower, kept telling him it was a purely political situation, but MacArthur treated the starving veterans as an enemy force.

Manchester also documents MacArthur's readiness to flout regulations and disobey instructions, particularly his penchant for making political pronouncements, and his animus toward military administrators and superiors, beginning with the colonels like George C. Marshall at Pershing's headquarters, who seemed ever ready to cut him down and hold him back. In short, the psyche within this dazzling military personality lived aloof in its own dramatic world, unique, not part of a team or community. By comparison, Mao Tse-tung and other world shakers seem lacking in self-confidence. Egotism made MacArthur tick. The fact that it ultimately torpedoed him like a Greek king hit by hubris is only incidental. Egotism helped him to do the unexpected in battle, play the hero, and rule Japan. But it put off the press, many of his peers, and the American public.

MacArthur attracted some devoted followers, wangled his way in military politics, but fared poorly in public controversies. While superintendent of West Point in 1922 he married a millionairess, Louise Cromwell Brooks, in whom the chief of staff, Pershing, was also interested. For this he was ostracized by Pershing with a tour in the Philippines (where he mapped the Bataan peninsula). But Louise divorced him in 1929. Unlike Douglas, she had a sense of humor. As she later told a Georgetown neighbor (my mother), "When Doug was striding about upstairs practicing a speech, I called up to him, 'When you want applause, flush the toilet.' 'Don't be vulgar,' he said." During the 1948 election she told a reporter, "If he's a dark horse, he's in the last roundup."

Under Roosevelt, to whom he seemed as dangerous as Huey Long, MacArthur set up the Civilian Conservation Corps with his usual efficiency. But when Pershing phoned him from retirement to urge a star for George C. Marshall, he appointed Colonel Marshall instead to be the instructor of the Illinois National Guard. After four years as chief of staff, trying to preserve the bare bones of a skeleton army, MacArthur went off to head a U.S. military mission to the Philippines, with Eisenhower still his chief assistant. After the Philippines became a commonwealth, MacArthur became its first field marshal and resigned from the American army's active list. His mother had died, and he married another Southerner, Jean Faircloth, whose grandfather had been one of the defenders of Missionary Ridge. She gave him complete support and a son named Arthur MacArthur IV.

His American Caesarism had two opportunities to flourish— when he commanded the Southwest Pacific theater from 1941 to 1945, and when he was Supreme Commander for the Allied Powers (SCAP) in Japan between 1945 and 1951. In both these posts he controlled the ingress of persons, tried to manage the outflow of news, planned his operations and worked his staff with great effectiveness, and in short dominated the action as the military commander. Thus he kept the Office of Strategic Services out of his theater entirely and kept the Office of War Information's nominal representative at his headquarters so disciplined that when we finally got him to a conference in Washington, he said nothing.

MacArthur's theater received minimal supplies. "Never was the Southwest Pacific allocated as much as 15 percent of the American war effort." Yet he made eighty-seven amphibious landings, all successful, and his casualties in the two years of fighting between Australia and the Philippines totaled 27,684, which may be compared with 72,306 at Anzio alone and 28,366 in Normandy. (That "he" did all this is the way he thought about it to himself and the way he got it put into the news record and into the public mind.)

"New weapons," said MacArthur, "require new and imaginative methods." Except early on at Buna, he avoided the slugging matches that killed so many U.S. Marines on Guadalcanal and Iwo Jima in the navy's sector of operations. Instead, MacArthur practiced "leapfrogging," a new form of enveloping the enemy by sea and air power. Manchester brings out the fact that bypassing the hundred thousand Japanese dug in at Rabaul was probably Marshall's idea. But once started, MacArthur leaped to the Admiralties, to Hollandia, and eventually to Leyte. Alanbrooke, Liddell Hart, and others agree that his generalship "outshone Marshall, Eisenhower, and all the other American and British generals including Montgomery."

In Manchester's study of the major controversies, MacArthur

comes off better than he has usually been pictured. To be sure, his planes were caught on the ground on Pearl Harbor Day, as though the Japanese surprise had disoriented him (like Stalin, no doubt, when Hitler attacked). But his withdrawal to Bataan was skillfully done, except for the neglect of food supplies, and on Corregidor, where he stood outside to watch the Japanese bombers, he became firmly resolved to die with his men. Churchill, Roosevelt, and Marshall were convinced by Australian Prime Minister Curtin that MacArthur must be brought out to defend Australia (otherwise Curtin would withdraw the three Australian divisions from El Alamein, opening Egypt to Rommel). When he left his troops under Wainwright on Bataan, it was MacArthur's one bitter defeat. He said "I shall return," he named his plane *Bataan,* and when he took Japan's surrender on the *Missouri* in Tokyo Bay, Wainwright, though much thinner, was beside him.

Once the Japanese were on the defensive, MacArthur's chief competitors were Nimitz and the navy. The navy's success with its carriers, driving straight for Japan, had already bypassed Stilwell's war to stabilize China as a base for bombing Japan, and as our bombing technology continued to develop, MacArthur's theater was also in danger of becoming a strategic sideshow. It was saved from this partly by Marshall, a war planner unencumbered by vanity or self-concern. The issue whether to take Luzon or Formosa (Taiwan), as advocated respectively by MacArthur and by Nimitz, was resolved when they met with FDR in Honolulu in July 1944. Manchester accepts the suggestion of the historian D. Clayton James that President Roosevelt and General MacArthur, whose presidential hopes had already been dashed, made an informal or implicit deal, that MacArthur's triumphant return to the Philippines would come in time to bolster FDR's fourth-term election in November. It came, at any rate, in October.

MacArthur began his shogunate in Japan by landing essentially unarmed and unprotected at Atsugi airport, the old kamikaze training base outside Yokohama, amid rumors that some of these diehard fanatics were waiting for him. Churchill called this the bravest of "all the amazing deeds in the war." He found thirty thousand Japanese troops with fixed bayonets lining his path into the city with their backs to him, as if for the emperor. Like nearly all his other calculated risks, this one worked too. One of his motives, inherited from West Point, was to keep ahead of the U.S. Navy, whose admirals were flocking ashore at Yokohama.

In the occupation MacArthur's Supreme Command was guided by the initial postsurrender directives worked out by Japan specialists like Hugh Borton of the State Department, but Manchester's colorful account leaves this matter obscure. We are confronted with the paradox that the MacArthur who brought oligarchic collaborators like Roxas and Laurel back into power in the unrevolutionized Philippines somehow became a social-minded liberal when he moved a thousand miles north. It is only realism to note that he had full instructions on what to aim at in the occupation, and it was not a one-man job—although like all MacArthur operations it may have seemed so from a distance. Indeed, the fascination of MacArthur studies, which will have a continuing future, lies in the way this imperious, ready-to-die virtuoso out of the American army fitted into the Japanese need for authority in adversity.

The shogunal tradition for almost seven hundred years until 1868 had allowed a conquering warrior's descendants to rule Japan in the emperor's name. How MacArthur and the part he played fitted with Japanese history and culture is a further question. So is the planning that fed into SCAP, the question of MacArthur's relations with his variegated staff, how land reform got going under the American agricultural expert Wolf Ladejinski, and how the MacArthur constitution was really put together. These are all matters of a different, more analytical order than MacArthur's fast-paced career. Never mind. Hubris is yet to come.

It was prepared for by MacArthur's Inchon landing, which in September 1950 enveloped and destroyed the North Korean forces that had overrun South Korea after June 25. Inchon, the harbor for Seoul, was a mud flat passable for modern vessels only during the thirty-two-foot high tides of September 15 or September 27, and then only at dawn or dusk. Every admiral and general who heard of MacArthur's plan to land at Inchon considered it insane, until he addressed them in convocation: if they were so against it, he argued, then the Koreans too would not expect it. The landing worked, Seoul was recovered, and MacArthur was a genius more than ever. The United Nations' invasion of North Korea began in this euphoria. Crossing the thirty-eighth parallel was not just MacArthur's idea; Marshall as secretary of defense gave it the green light, and the UN General Assembly endorsed it forty-seven to five.

When President Truman, unaccompanied by Marshall or the chiefs of staff, flew to Wake Island to see MacArthur on October 1, the general was ambushed. Truman's motive was political, to get public support for the congressional elections; the "off-the-record" discussion was recorded by a hidden stenographer and later used by Truman. Douglas MacArthur and the onetime artillery captain did not see eye to eye. After the Chinese intervention stalemated the Korean War, MacArthur wanted to expand it and flouted orders by taking his case directly to the American people in unauthorized policy statements. He even spoiled Truman's well-prepared effort for a truce and was quite properly cashiered for insubordination on April 10, 1951. The policy issue turned on the desirability of limited war—whether to accept stalemate as a substitute for victory, thus avoiding expansion of the war and the use of nuclear weapons. The military daring that MacArthur personified had been outdated by the atom bomb. Mr. Manchester carries his colorful story through to MacArthur's funeral in 1964, but has rather little to offer on his career's significance, or even on the motives of his climactic insubordination.

Since the inhibition to use nuclear weapons has lasted for forty years, while wars and armaments have continued to be major investments worldwide, we are plainly in a new era. Setting an example of personal courage in the face of enemy fire is no longer a possibility for general officers. Even enveloping the enemy by sea and air power may be as ineffectual as it proved to be in Vietnam (although one cannot help wondering what MacArthur might have done there with, say, two thousand helicopters). Consequently a reader who responds to MacArthur's daring feats and to his patriotic rhetoric can only conclude that we are now in serious trouble. Human impulses toward righteous combat in defense of freedom and staking all to achieve the glory of victory don't seem adequate to our needs any more. Yet MacArthur made history with them not very long ago, and just after his death, though contrary to his advice to both Eisenhower and Kennedy, we followed the martial impulse into another limited war in Vietnam and met frustrations even greater than those MacArthur's romantic egotism could not abide in Korea. Can we put his brilliant military example behind us and keep it there?

PART TWO

Penetrating Mao's China

The projection of American values abroad is nowhere better illustrated than in the American public's changing image of Mao
and the revolution in China. When seen factually as an aspiration
of underdogs to liberate the Chinese people, the revolution finds
American sympathy. When viewed, however, as an example of totalitarian communism on the march, it becomes an ideological
menace. Admiration and fear make for a strong ambivalence. All
reports from China are measured by this double yardstick, which
leads to a good deal of confusion and altercation, both among
observers and among the American public.

Some say the American reaction to the Chinese Communist Revolution shows the kind of "liberal fallacy" that sometimes befogs
American expansion on the march in strange places overseas.
When a noncommunist government is on "our side" rather than
the "other side," we hope it will measure up to our ideals. We tend
to take it into the American family like another state of the union,
and so we deplore evidence of corruption, secret-police terrorism,
censorship of the press, and any other infractions of human rights.
In contrast, when we look at a communist state, we are generally
unable to mount such criticisms because no news comes out and
we have less to exemplify the frustration of our ideals. Some say
this sets up a double standard. We castigate a "friendly" government for its torture of dissidents and similar crimes, whereas we
have less to say, because we lack the information, about the widespread torture and execution under a communist regime. This ar-
gument is superficially appealing, especially to persons who think
only in terms of power politics. Yet it is fatally flawed the moment
one considers human motivation as a decisive factor in power
building and power holding. A dictatorship that lacks popular sup-

port may be a good candidate for communist-led rebellion and takeover. If human rights are an essential ingredient of our cause, and if we believe more is at stake in the world than mere power politics, we have to react to evil conduct wherever we find it.

These motifs are illustrated in public attitudes toward the Chinese Communists. When American military observers and journalists in Yenan in 1944 first encountered the Maoist leadership, it seemed truly "democratic" in style and quite admirable in its determination to liberate the Chinese common people not only from the Japanese invaders but from the social evils of landlordism, disease, ignorance, and poverty. Our allies in Chungking under Chiang Kai-shek and his crumbling administration could only gnash their teeth at the American liberal idealization of Yenan. Our impression of Nationalist Chinese ineptitude and superior Chinese Communist effectiveness was confirmed by the civil war. The Chinese Communist takeover of China in 1949 and later, as far as we could see it, seemed a model of patriotic efficiency and devotion to revolutionary ideals for the betterment of the Chinese people and the strengthening of the state. We did not know the number of people they executed.

As of 1950, however, we found ourselves fighting the Chinese "volunteers" in Korea, and the cold war was teaching us to distrust their propaganda, fear their potential, and cling to our Nationalist ally on Taiwan. This swing of the pendulum lasted through the cold-war era down to the thaw in Sino-American relations in about 1970. Our first journalistic forays into Mao's China in the wake of Henry Kissinger in 1971, and President Nixon's grandstand play in meeting with Mao and Chou in February 1972, ushered in a new phase of euphoria that tapered off after the death of Mao in 1976.

Plainly, in 1971–1972 we faced a considerable problem. How from superficial observation could we get a realistic view of the facts of life in China? Our first impressions barely scratched the surface.

9

First Impressions, 1971–1972

In the news and propaganda cold war between communism and the free press in the United States, the resumption of Sino-American relations handed us a signal defeat. Our best-qualified observers went to Peking in late 1971 before the Nixon visit of February 1972, and then with Mr. Nixon went our top commentators on evening television. Yet all this combined talent was unable to pick up any newsworthy indication of the Cultural Revolution. It happened that this attack by Chairman Mao on university professors and professional writers and artists, together with bureaucrats in the party and government, had reached a particularly venomous climax in 1971–1972. Although the Cultural Revolution had been officially declared at an end in April 1969, the brutal ferreting-out of suspects together with the forcing of confessions under torture and numerous executions all were still going on under the direction of the army, which had been called in to keep order when all else failed. In those years the intellectuals who had been rusticated, sent to labor camps, or simply imprisoned were still for the most part undergoing that treatment. When my wife and I visited Peking in May–June of 1972, we saw a few old friends among the Chinese intellectuals but they said nothing

This chapter is derived in part from a review of Tillman Durdin, James Reston, and Seymour Topping, with Audrey Topping, *The New York Times Report from Red China*, ed. Frank Ching (New York: Quadrangle Books, 1972), and of Klaus Mehnert, *China Returns* (New York: Dutton, 1972), that appeared as "Getting to Know You" in the *New York Review of Books*, February 24, 1972; and in part from a review of Shirley MacLaine, *You Can Get There from Here* (New York: Norton, 1975), that appeared as "Numero Uno" in the *New York Review of Books*, May 1, 1975. Reprinted with permission from the *New York Review of Books*. Copyright © 1972, 1975 Nyrev, Inc.

to us about the Cultural Revolution. Others, we understood, were out of town or on trips and in any case unavailable.

The fact is that the most experienced American observers got no inkling and reported no news of what is now seen as a great watershed or climax of the revolution under Mao. To judge by reports published ten years later, several hundred thousand victims had been harassed, "struggled with" in meetings, beaten, tortured, and in some cases killed or allowed to commit suicide. Some estimates put the number of victims at roughly a million, although the criteria, like the facts themselves, are hard to pin down. Chinese intellectuals of today portray this era as the lowest point of their experience, yet the American press and observers remained entirely unaware of it. The horror stories finally began to leak out via Hong Kong and via Europeans with intellectual contacts.

In the shadow of this circumstance it is sobering to see the variety of responses by Americans to the revolutionary China with which they were once again in touch. They were not, of course, primarily interested in the intellectuals.

•   •   •

Three highly skilled *New York Times* reporters visited China in succession between April and August 1971. They reported, in effect, that the Chinese Communist Revolution seemed to have been a success, a good thing on balance for the long-suffering Chinese people and no particular harm to us. While our two decades of suspicion and hostility toward China would wear off only slowly, those years seem from these reports to have been still another wasted investment in the take-no-chances kind of security policy, the hyperactive defense, that our technology makes so feasible. As James Reston wrote from Shanghai in August, "The Chinese attitudes and approach to life make one wonder why Washington was so worried about an aggressive and expansionist China. They are . . . more inward-looking than any major nation on earth . . . Long before the United States tried to 'contain' China, they were self-contained, quite satisfied that they had enough land, resources, and people."

Harrison Forman, one of the war correspondents allowed to visit Yenan in 1944, felt then that Mao and his colleagues had a promising future. Twenty-eight years later *The New York Times*

Report from Red China confirmed that view. "Red China" was still in red on the dust jacket, for the benefit of oldsters who hadn't caught up with the *Times*'s foreign policy, but the People's Republic was also mentioned (in smaller type). The back jacket showed Scotty Reston and Chou En-lai seated side by side, trading policies. Their exchange of August 9, filling twenty-six pages, was highly informative, unlike the nonreport of the twenty hours of Kissinger-Chou talks a month earlier. The fact was that intellectuals still being victimized in Cultural Revolution style were only a small part of the Chinese scene.

Tillman Durdin had had fifteen years' experience reporting on China before Mao came to power, and Seymour Topping saw China in World War II and after. His wife, Audrey, who contributed ten of the eighty dispatches and most of the photographs, had the merit of being a daughter of Canadian diplomat Chester Ronning and of having been in China in 1946–1948 and again in 1966. Since Reston had previously talked with everybody's leaders except the Chinese, one could hardly have picked a better team for a quick appraisal.

Durdin, comparing the new and the old like a sinological Rip Van Winkle, found no sign of ancestor reverence or religious observances, no women using cosmetics, no old literature or drama, no gaudy weddings or funerals. "Even the manners and attitudes of the people seem changed . . . People seem more direct and less polite." Durdin reiterated that the international group of journalists that he traveled with "had no contacts with people except through interpreters on conducted tours to places regularly shown to foreigners." On the other hand, Audrey Topping went with her father in May to his missionary birthplace, Fancheng, in Hupeh province 175 miles northwest of Wuhan, and they found the population grown from 40,000 to 189,000, with some 200 factories large and small, and 38 middle schools with 13,000 students. A new China indeed.

The general impression of these highly qualified observers was of a people now mostly young and certainly self-confident, well-organized, and intently at work on community problems of material production, health, literacy, and technological improvement. The old core cities were shabby, the new factory suburbs very plain but more livable, the villages the main focus of concern. There

Maoism was making the peasant into a citizen, politically active and responsible. Transport was still back in the age of the railway, bus, and bicycle. Public health programs used Western and Chinese medicine and tried to reach the village masses, eliminate disease, and slow down population growth. The economic effort was to keep industry decentralized and to manufacture consumer goods as far as possible at the commune level. Building on the old market areas of groups of villages in the countryside, the village production teams and brigades within a commune aimed at local self-sufficiency as part of China's general self-sufficiency. What was Mr. Dulles so worried about?

In Peking Reston felt "constantly reminded here of what American life must have been like on the frontier a century ago . . . This country is engaged in one vast cooperative barn-raising . . . They remind us of our own simpler agrarian past." This was appealing but carried little message for the Sino-American future.

It seemed that our two civilizations would continue to coexist, one extolling civil liberties and the other self-sacrifice, one denouncing the police state and the other individualism. Neither the teachings of Mao Tse-tung nor those of the U.S. Information Service could be expected to sweep both rice-paddy China and automobilized America into a homogenized new world. Americans would continue to believe in expansion—whether we call it the conversion of the world in this generation or free enterprise putting men on the moon—and the Chinese, who invented ancestor worship, bureaucracy, and the examination system so long ago, would continue to put their faith in social organization.

A firsthand appreciation of these cultural differences and before-and-after contrasts is what put the *New York Times* reporters so far ahead of the United States government in its effort to appraise China's realities. The counterparts of the *Times*'s Durdin were the Foreign Service officers in China whom Mr. Nixon led the way in purging thirty-five years ago—men like John Carter Vincent, O. Edmund Clubb, John Paton Davies, and John Stewart Service, who had they not resigned or been dropped in midcareer could have given the White House a useful perspective not derived from studies of Europe.

Since shifting to academia Mr. Clubb has published two major works on China's modern history, the later of which, *China and*

Russia, The Great Game (New York: Columbia University Press, 1971), puts current Sino-Soviet relations into the context of the long and complex relationship between the two empires. Mr. Davies' memoirs are in *Dragon by the Tail* (New York: Norton, 1972), and Mr. Service has published an illuminating analysis of the brief honeymoon period of first contact at Yenan in 1944, *The Amerasia Papers: Some Problems in the History of U.S.-China Relations* (Berkeley: University of California, Center for Chinese Studies, 1971), when Mao and Chou raised the possibility of a working relationship with the United States. In January 1945 they even asked about coming to see FDR to plan the details of military cooperation against Japan. Grateful as we may be for these works of historical hindsight, it would have been even more gratifying to have had one of the authors on our team in Peking during the week of February 21, 1972. It is safe to say, for example, that not one of these officers, had he been asked in 1965, would have accepted the thesis that Asians can be judiciously bombed to the conference table.

While Durdin and the Toppings could give us before-and-after appraisals, the German journalist Klaus Mehnert offered the American public a before-during-and-after view, in addition to a Sino-Soviet comparison. Mehnert was in fact uniquely quadricultural. Born in Moscow of German parents, he spent the early 1930s in Russia; the later 1930s in Berkeley and Honolulu, marrying an American; and the early 1940s in Shanghai, editing a journal. He had seen China first in 1929 and 1936, and returned again in 1957. In 1971, with the aid of his friend Prince Sihanouk, he spent a month traveling through fourteen provinces early in the year before the ping-pong breakthrough.

As a solitary West German visitor who was afforded special opportunities, Mehnert traveled some three thousand miles, hardly seeing another Westerner, and visited not only Canton, Shanghai, Hangchow, Nanking, and Peking, but also Sian, Yenan, Tachai in Shansi province, and certain model institutions. He pursued some questions, like the incentive system, relentlessly; and since his reports were not restricted like those of the *Times* to a few hundred words, his account was fuller and more penetrating. If the American journalists seemed to outshine the State Department, they in turn were outdistanced by Klaus Mehnert. This is principally because his close familiarity with the Soviet system added to his perspective on China. He was more versed in the ideological issues between the two communisms and could more readily see China in both Soviet and Maoist terms.

During one twenty-hour day in the famous Tachai Village or "Brigade" in Shansi, he found that among its 83 families and 420 persons there were 150 full-time workers, with 100 beasts of burden, 150 pigs, and 400 sheep on 53 acres of land. The countrywide slogan "Learn from Tachai!" which had brought in 4.5 million visitors, was inspired by the villagers' self-reliance in rebuilding after a flood catastrophe in 1963. By 1971 they had even set up a couple of electrically powered aerial tramways for transport up the loess terraces. Mehnert concluded that the secret of Tachai was simply "work, work, and more work"—not for money but for "the honor of Chairman Mao and our socialist fatherland." Workers banked some savings but didn't know the interest rate. Strong men got ten work points a day; strong women, being less muscular, got seven. These were not day wages, daily recorded, but salary levels set by discussion at an annual village assembly, taking due account of "political consciousness." (Alas, post-Mao revelations tell us Tachai was a false front, not what it claimed to be. For example, some of the work was done by soldiers. Mao's Potemkin village is now disesteemed.)

Northeast of Peking Mehnert visited a May Seventh cadre school, where city bureaucrats and intellectuals went to engage in physical labor and so get "closer to the masses." Here were 1,255 men and women, cadres and cultural workers. The bare summary of this group's reclaiming waste land, building wells and dwellings, setting up brick and metal can factories, conveyed a very bleak picture of inefficient hard work punctuated by Mao study and development of "revolutionary consciousness" by cleaning latrines and carting night soil. All this can be understood only if one envisages the immemorial ruling class prerogatives of the old Chinese literati, which were attacked in the Cultural Revolution.

Mehnert found Russia and China no longer comparable. One was industrialized and run by technicians, the other agrarian and antiexpert. He saw the USSR as a society now geared to individual achievement and consumption, China as a society geared to egalitarianism and production. Soviet hierarchy and bureaucratism contrasted with Chinese decentralization and spontaneity. But the Soviet Union was becoming less ideological and more open to foreign contact, whereas China in 1971 remained closed off, devoted to activist self-help and to Mao's continuing revolutionary effort against the rise of new privilege. Mehnert doubted that the selfless Maoist man could soon be created. But he worried about "the ease with which the attitudes of the Chinese can be manipulated." (The cult of Mao, which he found ubiquitous, has of course now been destroyed.)

What do less qualified American leaders make of Mao's China? The unusual national program of inviting foreign guests to see the fruits of revolution produced a spate of books. At the "China-to-me" end of the spectrum were the reactions of Shirley MacLaine. The first half of *You Can Get There from Here* recounts her vicissitudes in Hollywood, television, and the McGovern campaign, all of which illustrated those evils of individualism, sexuality, and bourgeois commercialism that the Maoist revolution sought at all costs to avoid. In late 1971 MacLaine was invited by the foreign minister in Peking, Ch'iao Kuan-hua (who must have been a cryptosociologist interested in human experimentation) to bring to China a group of twelve American women. The delegation that went to China in April 1973 could not have been more diverse if they had come from Mrs. Noah's ark: "a 200-pound, coal black woman of mammoth heart" from Mississippi, one Wallaceite from Texas, one Navaho, a twelve-year-old Racine schoolgirl, a starchy Republican, some academics, and a camera crew, "all feminists, but they were also individuals with their own special personalities and concerns."

Set down unprepared on the tour route in China, these mixed American personalities tended to fall ill of exhaustion and culture shock. China "got to them." Their bodies were in Shanghai, but their minds were still in the United States. As their leader said, "I talked with people about religion, death, marriage, money and happiness, and all the while I was trying to figure out their New Society." In the end they brought back a variety of messages and no doubt left their Chinese hosts confirmed in Mao's thought that "revolution is justified."

Shirley MacLaine decided that China's revolutionary accomplishments could not be due simply to the proletarian dictatorship.

"There was something else going on here. People related to each other in a way that I had never seen before." She felt this was a result of the system of self-criticism and so speculated on the effect self-criticism would have on individual creative expression. "Perhaps honest group communication reduced the need for individualistic artistic expression in the New Society." She contrasted China with "America's climate of anger, violence, crime, and corruption, . . . and her free-wheeling abuse of freedom." A year later MacLaine opened in Las Vegas: "China makes you believe that everything is possible."

10

Mao's Labor Camps

In the global community of the post–cold-war world, freedom of individual expression has become a universal problem like food and energy. It has been at issue on the Watergate and other fronts in the United States, and on the Sakharov-Solzhenitsyn front in Moscow, but will there be any Chinese Sakharovs? China is achieving technological development without political expression for the individual technician. The degree of individual freedom to be expected in the world's crowded future is more uncertain in China than in most places because the Chinese are so well organized and so anti-individualist in custom and doctrine. Are they going to prove individualism out of date?

China is usually fitted into the international world either by a theory of delayed progress or by a theory of uniqueness. The first theory assumes that China has merely been slow to get on the path of modernity, but once launched will come along like the rest of us with industrialization and its accompanying ills and triumphs. The second theory, which of course is the stock in trade of most China specialists, is that China is unique and will never be like other countries. (Since China is obviously both like and unlike other places, this whole discussion is a great semi-issue in which each contestant must make his own mixture.)

The view that China must follow universal laws of development,

This review of Bao Ruo-wang (Jean Pasqualini) and Rudolph Chelminski, *Prisoner of Mao: A Survivor's Account of the State Prison System of the New China* (New York: Coward, McCann & Geoghegan, 1973), appeared under the title "In Chinese Prisons" in the *New York Review of Books,* November 1, 1973. Reprinted with permission from the *New York Review of Books.* Copyright © 1973 Nyrev, Inc.

which appeals to Marxists among others, can lead one to conclude that China's growth in modern scientific scholarship still lags behind that of the Soviet Union, and so cases like that of academician Sakharov have not yet emerged in China but will do so in the future. Eventually, it may be assumed, a specialized scholarly elite cannot help having individual views and speaking out; but the People's Republic is still at the stage of its evolution where egalitarianism is the dominant creed, education is to be only a matter of acquiring technical skills for public purposes, and in order to avoid the revival of the old ruling class tradition no scholarly elite can be allowed to grow up in the universities. By this reckoning China, like the USSR, is on our track but has a long way still to go.

If one takes the other tack stressing the special character of Chinese society, one may conclude that the Chinese are far more sophisticated in their social organization and political life than we distant outsiders commonly realize. This view is compatible with the Maoist orthodoxy in China, which claims that the Soviets have lost the true communist vision, whereas China retains it and can avoid the evils of capitalism including the American type of individualism.

From either point of view China is seen to be setting a new style, achieving her own new solutions in applying technology to modern life. For example, helped by the press of numbers which makes cars for individuals inconceivable, the Chinese may escape the corrosive effects of automobile civilization. In such a crowded country, communities cannot be easily destroyed, and the apparent high morale of villagers in the countryside betokens a people who can absorb a great deal more modern technology without having their local society disrupted.

In this view China is well rid of the Western type of individual political expression, opposed to it both because of tradition and because of present-day circumstances. Life in China will follow norms other than the Bill of Rights because the letter of the law and litigation through due process are still less esteemed than the common moral sense and opinion of the group, subordinating individual interests to those of the community. The mass of China is dense enough to permit this new Maoist way of life to be preserved during industrialization, in spite of some growth of international contact through guided tourism. Given their numbers, resources, and traditions, the Chinese are obliged to create their own novel anti-individualist society. No one else has a model for them to follow, although the Soviets have offered them the most.

Nevertheless, Western word users of all sorts who appreciate their relative freedom of expression will continue to scan the variegated flood of China books for clues to the future of individualism there. Are all Chinese dutiful and interchangeable parts of a huge production machine? What is the role of dissent in the society? What are its limits? How are dissidents handled?

China's treatment of deviant individuals in labor camps owes something to Soviet inspiration, but has developed in the Chinese style, not the Soviet. The contrast emerges from an unusual survivor account by a Franco-Chinese who got the full treatment during seven lean years, but learned how to survive in the system and was discharged when France recognized China in 1964. His account is more than twenty years old, from the time of troubles before the Cultural Revolution.

Jean Pasqualini was born in China in 1926 of a French Army father and a Chinese mother. He grew up with Chinese playmates, looking Chinese and speaking like a native. He learned French and English at French Catholic mission schools, and held the passport of a French citizen resident in China. In 1945 he worked for the Fifth U.S. Marines as a civilian specialist with the military police, and later for the U.S. Army Criminal Investigation Division until November 1948. In 1953 he got a job in a Western embassy in Peking and finally was arrested during the Anti-Rightist Campaign in December 1957.

Under his Chinese name, Bao Ruo-wang, he spent seven years of a twelve-year sentence for criminal activities in the Chinese Communist labor camps, one of many millions undergoing Reform through Labor (*Lao Gai* or *Lao-tung kai-tsao*), to be distinguished from the other multitudes undergoing Reeducation through Labor (*Lao Jiao* or *Lao-tung chiao-yang*). After de Gaulle's recognition of the People's Republic in 1964 led to Bao's release, he went to Paris for the first time, where he is today a respected teacher of the Chinese language.

In 1969 Rudolph Chelminski, a *Life* correspondent in Paris who had just spent two years in its Moscow bureau, heard Pasqualini's amazing stories. The two men began a three-year spare-time collaboration, which produced *Prisoner of Mao*. Chelminski soon "realized (to my surprise, I admit) that neither Jean nor the book we were developing was anti-Chinese or even anticommunist, in the camps he had been frankly employed as slave labor, and yet he couldn't fail to admire the strength of spirit of the Chinese people and the honesty and dedication of most of the communist cadres he met."

The book is indeed unique, probably a classic. Like William Hinton's 1966 book, *Fanshen: A Documentary of Revolution in a Chinese Village,* the story has been skillfully put together with conversations, personalities, and incidents made clear-cut and dramatic. It invites comparison with the accounts of Soviet labor camps, and the comparison goes in China's favor. Pasqualini recounts a harrowing ordeal in grim detail, but it is set in a social context of dedication to the revolution in word and deed. The individual is expected to submit completely and strive for reform, on the same ancient assumption that underlay Confucianism— that man is perfectible and can be led to proper conduct.

Pasqualini confirms the impression researchers gained from talking to Kwangtung escapees in Hong Kong, that the Chinese camps see little growth of an "inmate subculture." In modern American prisons, as also in Soviet labor camps under Stalin, the coercive nature of prison life creates an informal subculture that dominates the prisoners and hinders their rehabilitation. In the Stalinist case, little stress was put on political reeducation. Instead, the genuine criminals were put in charge of the political offenders—which possibly fostered production, but not reform.

These evils the Chinese avoided. Pasqualini says that Chinese camps are so effectively run that they make a profit; the Chinese, unlike the Soviets, realize that mere coercion cannot get the most productive performance from prisoners. The Chinese system in Pasqualini's time used hunger as a major incentive, plus mutual surveillance, mutual denunciation, and self-evaluation as automatic disciplinary measures. But the main emphasis, after labor, was on study and self-improvement. For most of the millions who enter the labor camps the experience, he says, is permanent; few ever return to civilian life. Instead, after their terms have expired they continue as "free workers" in the camp factory—with some extra privileges but under the same tight discipline, pretty thoroughly adjusted and continuously productive.

After his arrest Pasqualini—or Bao, to use his Chinese name— spent his first fifteen months in an interrogation center. Under the warders' close supervision, his dozen cellmates constantly exhorted one another to behave properly and with gratitude to the government for the chance to expiate their crimes and achieve reform. The government policy was "leniency to those who confess, severity to those who resist, expiation of crimes through gaining merits, reward to those who have gained merits." The key principle throughout was complete submission to authority.

Early on, Bao was led into a torture chamber full of grisly equipment, only to be told after his first shock that it was a museum preserved from the Kuomintang era. Throughout his experience physical coercion of prisoners was strictly forbidden. Prison life was thoroughly organized to occupy nearly every waking moment. Prisoners moved at a trot, with their heads bowed, looking neither right nor left. They followed punctilious daily routines, including periods for meditation when they sat cross-legged on their beds "exactly like a flock of Buddhist monks." Five days a week were occupied with confessions and interrogations, which each man worked out laboriously for himself with his interrogators. Bao wound up with a seven-hundred-page statement. Sunday was free for political study and Tuesday for cleanup, including passing around "a little box for toenail parings" collected monthly and sold for use in traditional Chinese medicine. The proceeds paid for a movie every four months. During fifteen months in this detention center Bao "ate rice only once and meat never. Six months after my arrest my stomach was entirely caved-in and I began to have the characteristic bruised joints that came from simple body contact with the communal bed." Vitamin deficiency led to his hair's falling out and his skin's rubbing off.

"Facing the government we must study together and watch each other" was the slogan posted on the walls. Occasionally the study session would be punctuated by a struggle meeting, "a peculiarly Chinese invention combining intimidation, humiliation and sheer exhaustion . . . an intellectual gang-beating of one man by many, sometimes even thousands, in which the victim has no defense, not even truth." A struggle can go on indefinitely until contrition has been achieved. The only way out is to develop a revolutionary ardor, and the only means for that is full confession. When it was decreed that all prisoners should take a two-hour nap in the summer afternoon, "anyone with his eyes open would receive a written reprimand. Enough reprimands and he would be ripe for struggling. We were very well-behaved. Model children."

When his interrogation was finally complete, Bao was shown the dossier of accusations against him. He found that all kinds of friends and colleagues had submitted their hand-written denunciation forms about him. It was now his turn to denounce others. "We want you to reform, but how can we consider you to be truly on the good road unless you tell us about your associates? Denunciation of others is a very good method of penance."

Another of the devices for inhibiting prisoner solidarity was the system by which cellmates were obliged to settle the ration due each member, based on his own proposal and everyone else's assessment and vote. No one could help a friend eat well, any more than he could avoid struggling against him with hateful denunciations.

Finally Bao came to trial. "You are not obliged to say anything. You will answer only when you are told to. We have chosen someone for your defense." The defense lawyer made a simple point: "The accused has admitted committing these crimes of his own free will. Therefore no defense is necessary."

While awaiting sentence Bao was transferred to a transit center known as the Peking Experimental Scientific Instruments Factory, situated next to the pretty Tao Ran Ting Park. Here he found that productive labor consisted in folding three-foot-by-two-foot printed sheets three times onto themselves to make book pages. The communal plank beds that nightly held twelve men side by side were dismantled and used as work space by day. The beginner's norm of three thousand pages a day was difficult to achieve at first, but the average output was forty-five hundred and the target of the government was six thousand. One ate a ration according to one's performance. Beginners got about thirty-one pounds of food a month; folding three thousand pages a day got one forty-one pounds a month. Work was from 5:00 A.M. to 7:30 P.M. After a bit Bao got up to thirty-five hundred pages a day; his weight, however, dropped to 110 pounds. By the time he left the transit center he had few fingernails left but he was folding up to ten thousand pages a day.

He finally received a sentence of twelve years' imprisonment for reform through labor. His experience was fairly straightforward, perhaps because of his foreign nationality. In many cases a sentence of, say, ten years for the record is not announced to the prisoner, who may be led to believe it is twenty years or life. Subsequently he is given apparent reductions of sentence. By the time he is said to have served his sentence and become a free worker, though still in the camps, he feels accumulated gratitude for these apparent reductions.

A year and a half after his arrest Bao had a six-minute visit from his wife and one of his children. After being thoroughly searched—the linings of jackets slit open with a razor blade—the prisoners receiving visitors were instructed to speak in a loud voice across the plank separating them. Even this was better than a "dishonorable visit," in which a recalcitrant prisoner was visited by family members brought specially to upbraid him and admonish him to improve his conduct.

Prisoners in the 1958–1959 period were caught up in the campaigns of the time. Urged to write down his feelings about his own sentence and crimes, Bao made the mistake of responding sincerely and stated that the government's alleged concern for him seemed to be a sham. All it really wanted from the prisoners was cheap slave labor. Soon this statement was used, at the end of the ideological reform campaign, to make him an example. He was put in chains in a solitary cell about four feet long and four and a half feet high, with room enough to sit but not to stand or lie down, and a permanently lit electric bulb overhead. At mealtime his handcuffs, which had been fastened behind him, were changed to the front, which was better than his having to lap up the food ration like a dog. With his hands bound, however, he could hardly fight off the lice that soon flourished on his body.

After five days he asked to speak with someone from the Ministry of Public Security, to whom he said that the government had told him lies when the warder had assured him that honesty would be rewarded and his worst thoughts should be put on paper. "Having obeyed because of my profound confidence in the government and the Party, I was now being rewarded with solitary. Where was my sin?" This got him out, since "the Maoist order is inordinately proud of its own special sort of integrity."

In September 1959 he was transferred to Peking Prison Number

One, the model jail where he found it "almost shocking to be treated like a human being." The food was good and plentiful, and the warden sympathetic and humane. "Maybe it was the classical Pavlovian approach . . . his decency after two years of pain and humiliation was absolutely inspirational." Here Bao put together his first full-scale ideological review. In this the principles of criticism and self-criticism are the same as for citizens outside. Confession should be spontaneous the moment one commits any error. Others should be quick to assist anyone who makes a mistake so that he can recognize it more readily. Only if this fails is the individual pushed into struggle or solitary. In this statement Bao typically declared that his sentence seemed most lenient and just, confessed that he had disregarded the regulations that prisoners should always move in groups of two or more because several times he had gone to the latrine alone, and other times in study sessions he had not sat in the regulation manner, or again he had talked during working hours. Worse, he had been reluctant to report on persons who had been good to him, although actually reporting on others is a "two-way help: it helps the government to know what is going on and it helps the person involved by making it possible for him to recognize his mistakes." He finally wound up pledging to listen to the government in all things. At this point he realized he was only protecting his skin, but "before I left the Chinese jails, I was writing those phrases and believing them." As one old-timer told him, "The only way to survive in jail is to write a confession right away and make your sins look as black as possible . . . but don't ever hint that the prison authorities or the government share any of the responsibility."

By this time Bao was diagnosed as having tuberculosis, so spent a couple of months in an infirmary. From there he went to the Ching Ho camp for an outdoor life in the fields. China was now entering the hard years of malnutrition, and the ration for prison farms naturally suffered. Bao found himself in a settlement of the old and weak, where discipline was less strict, there were few norms, and hardly any guards. As one of the ablebodied gang he worked on the pig manure detail and learned more about how to survive, for example by snuggling up to the pigs on cold nights.

With their low rations the prisoners he had seen thus far had never shown any sexual problems. But one day the camp barber was found to have seduced a feebleminded young prisoner. Within hours the barber was brought in front of the assembly, denounced, condemned, and shot, his brains spraying over the front rows of the audience. "I have read of men being raped in Western prisons. In China the guilty party would be shot on the spot."

In October Bao went with a selected group on the long trip to the northeast as a volunteer for the famous Hsing Kai Hu farm in the barren lands north of Harbin on the Soviet frontier. "Everything seemed abundant up here in Manchuria and strangely unprisonlike." The vast confines of the camp area encompassed fields, barracks, watchtowers, villages. "Everything seemed orderly and well-tended." The inhabitants welcomed the newcomers like human beings. The food seemed first-rate. "Improper attitude rather than low production was the criterion for cutting a man's rations . . . After a few days in the fields I was truly happy to be in the barren lands." Unfortunately, it was found that he was a foreigner in a sensitive frontier area. Together with a couple of overseas Chinese he was sent back to Ching Ho after only a brief experience in this invigorating environment.

The fall of 1960 found Bao still struggling to get enough to eat as the winter cold came on. Work was reduced to six hours a day. Conditions became truly desperate as the food supply dwindled. The camp experimented with ersatz, in the form of paper pulp, mixed in the food. At first this made the steamed bread bigger and more filling, but soon the whole farm suffered "probably one of the most serious cases of mass constipation in medical history because the paper pulp powder had absorbed the moisture from the digestive tract . . . I had to stick my finger up my anus and dig it out in dry lumps like sawdust." Another effort was to use marsh water plankton but this proved unassimilable. Still, the warden was able to give them a New Year's meal with rice, meat, and vegetables.

By 1961 Bao had achieved a high ideological level: he believed what the warders told him, respected most of the guards, and was convinced that if the government didn't exactly love him it was at least doing everything within its power to keep him healthy in bad times. In this season of semistarvation the warders put rumors to rest by taking all the prisoners through their own kitchen to show that they too were living on sweet potato flour mixed with corncob ersatz. "Chinese communists are often painful fanatics but they are straight and honest."

As a foreigner, Bao realized he was the only one who stood any chance of ever getting out of China and therefore he had avoided breaking the rule against foraging for extra food. But he developed low blood pressure and other signs of vitamin deficiency. Now his cellmates taught him the tricks of foraging, stealing a turnip, or reconditioning the discarded outer leaves of cabbages to balance their diet. One of his cellmates gave him some corn that had a strange powerful taste like ammonia, foraged from horse droppings. By May 1961 he was ill and in the infirmary with amoebic dysentery and anemia, well on the way toward extinction. But cellmates kept bringing him special food, products of their foraging. After he had made it back to health and work again, one of them explained, "You're the only one who's different, Bao. You might get out the Big Door someday. It could happen to a foreigner but not us. You'll be the only one who can tell about it afterward."

When they got back to work in summertime in the paddyfields, it was possible to catch frogs. "We would skin them on the spot and eat them raw. The system is to start with the mouth and the head comes off with the spine."

One cold night, instead of going 200 yards to the latrine, Bao pissed against a wall. "I had barely finished when I received a very sharp and swift kick in the ass. It was a warder. 'Don't you realize the sanitation rules?' he demanded. He was quite right but it was the ass of an ideological veteran he had kicked. 'I admit I am wrong, Warder, but I had the impression that government members were not supposed to lay hands on prisoners. I thought physical violence was forbidden.'" The warder admitted his mistake, said he would bring it up at his next self-criticism session, and sent Bao back to his cell to write a confession. Bao thereupon confessed that his pissing on the wall had demonstrated "a disregard for the teachings of the government and a resistance to reform . . . displaying my anger in an underhanded manner . . . like spitting in the face of the government when I thought no one was looking. I can only ask that the government punish me as severely as possible." The result was no punishment.

By 1963 Bao was so ideologically active and correct that he was trusted to be a cell leader. "With the zeal of a true convert I began searching for new ways to serve the government and help my fellow men." Among other things he went barefoot in summertime to save the government shoe leather. Finally, however, he confessed to having bad thoughts: if Chinese consuls demanded access to their nationals in Indian camps (as they were doing just then), the French consul should have access to Bao in China. Bao said he knew such ideas were wrong, but still he had them. "I would not be sincere," he wrote, "if I kept them hidden from the government." His ideological reform seemed to have taken hold of him so completely that it probably contributed to his release as a French citizen when Sino-French diplomatic relations were established in 1964.

Other foreigners and Chinese who had lived abroad, as Bao had not, were unable to achieve his degree of conversion and acceptance. He records many bitter personal tragedies among this class of prisoners, whose foreign background made them eternally vulnerable.

Chinese intellectuals in general seemed unable sufficiently to abjure their individualism. "Like the Soviets, the Chinese ideologues cordially despise and mistrust the intelligentsia because of its irritating tendency to form its own ideas."

11

The Grip of History on China's Leadership

When we are unacquainted with a foreign culture, we seem condemned to understand it in light of our own. Peking politics is made more opaque to us by the Chinese terms it uses. China's political discourse is not only moralistic, it mixes together allusions to figures like the First Emperor of the Ch'in, founder of the unified empire in 221 B.C. (who may be regarded variously as a cruel tyrant or a progressive one), and recent Marxist-derived terms like "capitalist-roader" (a man who may be a faithful party member but still favors using material incentives to stimulate production; not a capitalist but someone heading in a materialistic direction). Between Chinese folklore and Marxism, both alien to the American mind, we confront a jumble of terms whose obvious vigor is matched only by their capacity to befuddle. Since Chinese political argumentation is usually indirect and allusive, its opacity is a measure of our own ignorance.

History can help us. To begin with, Mao Tse-tung and Chou En-lai, in addition to being the major leaders of the Chinese Communist Revolution, performed two typical historical roles, those of emperor and loyal minister. By the end of the Ch'ing dynasty in 1912, when Mao was an advanced teenager in school, the Chinese monarchy had evolved for more than two thousand years. Unfor-

Part of this chapter appeared in the *New York Review of Books,* May 1, 1975, as a review of *Chairman Mao Talks to the People, Talks and Letters: 1956–1971,* ed. Stuart Schram, trans. John Chinnery and Tieyun (New York: Pantheon, 1974). Reprinted with permission from the *New York Review of Books.* Copyright © 1975 Nyrev, Inc. The remainder of the chapter is from an article that appeared as "Peking Politics: A Westerner's Guide" in *Harvard Magazine,* September 1976.

tunately, our study of China is so underdeveloped that this, the world's oldest ruling institution, has not really been analyzed in political science terms even today—partly, no doubt, because the records are too extensive for historians and too difficult for political scientists. We know that the Chinese monarchy came out of the same political tradition that produced the examination system for the selection of talent. This was under the T'ang, two hundred years before Charlemagne tried to revive a central government in the West. Having been the inventor of bureaucracy almost a thousand years earlier, the Chinese state proceeded to create very sophisticated institutions for the exercise of central power. This mighty tradition, lasting into the twentieth century, overhangs Chinese politics even today.

Any great revolutionary wants to leave history behind and start afresh. But of all peoples the Chinese are far and away the most history conscious, and Mao's speeches were full of historical allusions. China's revolution is preeminently against the Chinese past, both feudal and imperialist. If we suppose that the new ideas of the revolution dominate conscious thought, what about the half or two-thirds (or 90 percent?) of human conduct that remains unconsciously habituated, adjusted to the perduring environment? Understandably, Mao inveighed against old ideas and practices. But how far was his own institutional role like that of the old emperors?

Consider, for example, continuity in power. During the span of our American history since 1607, China had two emperors, who each ruled for sixty years (K'ang-hsi, 1662–1722; Ch'ien-lung, 1736–1795). The Empress Dowager held power for more than forty years, 1861–1908. And then came Mao, the old lady's exact opposite in every conceivable way, except for longevity in power. Imagine if FDR were still in the White House, having been there continuously since 1932! Mao Tse-tung led China's revolution from 1935 on—some would claim from 1927. This says something about the Chinese readiness to accept a supreme personality—instead of our idea of the supremacy of law and due process.

Mao outshone all the emperors by being more creative. But he was also like the best of them in being the One Man at the top, the main font of wisdom and policy, yet antibureaucratic, unpredictable, and even capricious, withdrawn from sight for months and then reemerging like thunder and lightning. Can Chinese politics function without such a figure? Only a supreme personality of Son-of-Heaven proportions could twice in succession cashier his Number Two in the hierarchy (Liu Shao-ch'i in 1967, Lin Piao in 1971), like an emperor sacking his chief ministers, and yet bring back a cashiered Number Three like Deputy Premier Deng Xiaoping (Teng Hsiao-p'ing) all the while remaining Number One himself.

Until 1911 the Son of Heaven sat on top of a multilayered ruling stratum of officials, upper scholar gentry, and lower landlord-merchant gentry—a privileged elite, hardly 5 percent of the population. Mao's unprecedented attack on this old ruling-class tradition made him by volume the greatest emancipator of all time. But his unique status did not come out of a vacuum; it came out of history. In reviewing the struggle for liberation from the top of the T'ien-an Men in the heart of Peking, Mao stood on the same central axis as the Hall of Supreme Harmony, where the emperors once sat enthroned, only a few hundred yards inside the Forbidden City. Not by accident, this is the strongest vantage point from which to attack China's outworn past.

We may conclude, therefore, that many of the traits demonstrated by Chairman Mao as the top power holder in the Chinese Communist Party after 1935 and in the People's Republic of China after 1949 were derived from attitudes and practices of the Chinese past. The secret of his performance need not be sought only by speculative reference to his presumed but unreported regard for his mother or his much-touted rivalry with his father. Once he became the top figure in China, he was subject to the pull of traditions embedded in Chinese thought and practice over the millennia.

Typically, a Chinese emperor as Son of Heaven stood above the rest of mankind, answerable to his ancestors and to the grand principles of the polity and Confucian morality, but not easily contained or controlled by any human agency. The emperor was the final arbiter in the selection of talent for office; as the judge of men, he had to balance ability against loyalty and stand or fall by the performance of his officials. His actions were therefore unbounded by regulations. Representing the dynastic interest, he had to be a law unto himself, capricious, unpredictable, and ruthless. Officials might be dismissed for no reason (other than their excellence and the emperor's jealousy). Those who rose highest were in the most precarious position. They might wield the imperial power one day and be in chains or exile the next. The very uncertainty of the imperial favor was a device to keep officials on their best behavior.

For instance, specialists in administration have been fascinated to find that the Ch'ing emperors (1644–1912) devised a top-secret "eyes-only" communications system early in the eighteenth century. Palace memorials from officials all over the empire might be sent for opening by the emperor only, and his comments on the memorial could then be sent back for receipt only by the memorialist in person. Thus the Ch'ing emperor had his informants widespread among his bureaucrats almost before Western rulers had bureaucracies.

Chou En-lai stood forth as the ideal minister: loyal to Mao since 1935, selfless in his devotion to duty, flexible and pragmatic in administration, and charismatic in his capacity to influence Chinese and foreigners alike. Only a man of talent who had inherited the tradition of the duke of Chou (who dutifully wielded power on behalf of a boy emperor almost three thousand years ago) could have been prime minister of the People's Republic for a quarter of a century without forming his own faction. Chou En-lai succeeded in avoiding the Number Two position until the very end, but remained throughout the one individual able to settle differences, work out compromises, get things done, and keep the administration moving. Surely one key to his record was the capacity never to challenge the top authority and yet to save it from its excesses and reintegrate the administration when Maoist campaigns had torn it apart. The fact that Chou at the end began to stand forth as a leader of moderates against radicals suggests that even he could not forestall the decline of Mao's leadership. When both were still competent they made a balanced team, and retrospect will probably enhance Chou's contribution to the Mao-Chou combination.

The fact that both these leaders were members of the new revolutionary generation, pledged to the destruction of an old order and creation of a new one, does not by any means remove them from the grip of Chinese tradition. The whole Chinese Revolution has been a struggle against the past. Revolutionaries in contention have commonly used the past against one another. This continuity does not deny the innovations of recent times. But for an American public seduced by ideas of the perfectibility of man in a new environment and by simplistic doctrines of behaviorism—as though the past did not largely control the present—it seems hard to grasp. Just as the syntax of sentences is less changeable than their content, so the basic patterns of Chinese political life may persist when the substance of ideas and policies has been turned upside down. For example, the Confucian ideal of harmony extolled for so many centuries gave way under Mao to the Social Darwinist idea of struggle, imported from the West. But in both cases the ideas took the shape of an official orthodoxy, which China's widespread government cannot do without.

When we come to the "struggle between two lines" of recent decades, we face first of all a configuration visible in many revolutions and developing countries. On the one hand, there is the gradual evolution of technological development under the general heading of industrialization or, more broadly, the application of science to modern problems. On the other hand, there is the fervor of revolutionary effort that sees the struggle as a moral drama, the good revolution against the evils of the old order. In these terms, the moderates are "pragmatists," as newsmen like to label them, who seem to us somehow more knowable and preferable to the opposition "radicals" and their doctrinaire jargon. On the whole, we are able to understand the technological developers in spite of their socialist abhorrence of free corporate enterprise. Deng Xiaoping, with his disregard of whether a cat is black or white as long as it will catch mice, seems like an intelligible figure, whereas the radicals speak a wild language and seem bent only on power seizure or economic disruption.

At this point, however, we are in danger of leaving the Prince of Denmark out of our revolutionary *Hamlet*. For the Chinese Revolution is certainly social as much as economic, and its social target is the destruction of the old ruling-class tradition. One cannot appreciate this fact without reference to Chinese history, particularly China's early success in the creation of a ruling class that could almost monopolize literacy, the higher culture, office holding, and the amassing of wealth, while remaining no more than 5 or 10 percent of the population. The sophistication of this ruling class and its capacity to co-opt talent from the masses and maintain its status and traditions are among the great stories of social history.

Among other things, the Chinese ruling class produced the Chinese historical record. We have thus been obliged to see China's past mainly through ruling-class eyes. From this point of view, the great mass of the farming population remained largely unheard from, working, starving, or rebelling, as the case might be, but always subject to the manipulation and guidance of a small stratum who worked with their minds and ruled those who worked with their muscles.

Since this ancient ruling-class tradition was outworn by the twentieth century, one primary aim of the revolution has been to wipe out its system of elitism by spreading the privileges of literacy, learning, mobility, and political participation to the mass of the people. This is indeed a democratic revolution in the broad sense. Yet, ironically, in the very process of its fulfillment there comes from the new citizenry the old quest for rising in status and privilege to make one's way into an upper stratum. The fact is that the ideal of the old ruling class had penetrated the masses. The secret of its continuity was that it remained the goal for all talent within the population. Thus, talent today is easily seduced by ideas of hierarchic status and special perquisites. The very thing that the revolution in Mao's eyes had to expunge seemed to reappear in those who led the revolution. This accounts for Mao's belief that there had to be a continuing revolution, meaning a continuing series of campaigns sporadically trying to wipe out old evils. One can sympathize with an old man who in the 1960s saw privilege reappearing in the new bureaucracy. One can admire his inventive guile and finesse in fielding teenagers as Red Guards unexpectedly to attack the party headquarters and rout out his wayward comrades—the inconceivable act that still gives Moscow nightmares.

Having said all this, however, we must remember that the ideals of the Maoist revolution were not democratic in the American sense, since there was still such a high degree of manipulation of the populace. The Maoist faction skillfully took over the media and used them to carry on its righteous attack against capitalist-roaders and other monsters and freaks. But what was the Maoists' complaint?

Here the American observer is again baffled by a Chinese tradition that equates undesirable policy with bad morals. This is a feature of Chinese political thinking that has never been satisfactorily explained. It seems to derive from the great doctrine of the unity of theory and practice; that is, that conduct expresses character, that what one says should be manifest in what one does. Once this tradition became established, one could not make the Western distinction between policy and morality. On the contrary, a policy is part of an official's conduct. If his policy becomes disesteemed, then his moral character is similarly impugned. One result of this concept is that it is impossible to have a "loyal opposition," because a person who is opposed to one's policies is ipso facto opposed to one's character and one's self. One cannot make the pluralistic Anglo-Saxon distinction between loyalty to the chief of state and disagreement with his current policy.

In contemporary China, however, we see an even more startling tradition in action—the denunciation of the evil character of persons in power. This reminds one of the censors of the traditional empire, who had the function from early times of impeaching other officials and even remonstrating with the sovereign over his conduct. Censors were trained by their classical studies to assert the primacy of basic Confucian principles and attack all worldly or self-seeking deviations. As late as the 1870s and 1880s, chauvinist officials were memorializing the emperor to denounce all contact with foreigners and, specifically, all compromise with the French, with whom the Chinese were fighting on the frontier of Indochina. This ancient element in Chinese politics has been known as "pure discussion" (ch'ing-i). We can best think of it as corresponding to the strident Americanism or anticommunism of our own political scene, combined with the hellfire and brimstone of our older evangelism. The wielder of ch'ing-i puts himself in an unassailable theoretical position. Typically he is not in a position of responsibility himself. Against such critics one cannot win. On the other hand, the ruler is ill-advised to follow their advice except as a means of chastising or shaking up the bureaucracy.

The two lines in Chinese policy argumentation and the two camps that espouse them can hardly be compared with alternative national parties such as our Democrats and Republicans. The contrast is greater, between economic growth and social change, and between administrators getting on with human tasks and ideologists asserting claims of perfect principle. The administrators on the whole seem almost by definition to be in power in the government and in the armed services, while the ideologists have generally controlled the media. For this reason one cannot see a balance of power; the radicals obviously have the upper hand in words, but can seldom follow up with executive action.

All such efforts to understand Chinese politics suffer from the basic fault that they are made by analogy to our own experience. We must remember that the aims of the administrators and the pronouncements of the ideologues are both very different from their equivalents in the United States. For example, we are not a predominantly farming country with a tradition of close-knit, almost collective, life in the villages. We have not customarily left it to a small elite to manage the upper levels of our literate national life.

When Chairman Mao and Prime Minister Chou were in their heyday, the chairman could give his blessing to periodic campaigns for social change, while the prime minister kept the administration functioning. The end of this working alliance, so successful over so many years, left Chairman Mao and those around him without a balance wheel. Where formerly the great leader could preside over the two lines and push one line only periodically, the Maoist position became that of an embattled and strident faction. The situation deteriorated and left China prey to uncertainty. Nevertheless, two lines are represented in policy divisions, for they have come out of the dual nature of the Chinese Revolution as an effort to strengthen the Chinese state by economic modernization and at the same time to change the character of Chinese life by social revolution in favor of the common citizen. The fact that revolutions wax and wane does not invalidate their aims.

In the Chinese case, the dependence of central authority upon ideological orthodoxy and morale, especially among the ruling bureaucracies, makes China particularly vulnerable to the waxing-and-waning process. For a regime that rules by moral authority rather than by due process of law, the major calamity is demoralization and the corruption that comes with it. Yet the ideals of the revolution will not die, and periodic efforts to combat bureau-

12

The Search for Chinese Individualism

One flaw in a human rights foreign policy is that human rights are not as pervasive as human righteousness, and the self-esteemed revolutionaries who monopolize righteousness in Russia and China will reject American tutelage. But if the Kremlin leaders do it a bit defensively as Europeans once removed, the same cannot be expected of Peking. To rule by virtue of virtuous conduct was a Chinese specialty long before Christianity and Roman law taught us that individuals have immortal souls and civil liberties. Confucian morality stressed duties, not rights, as the glue of social harmony, and individualism is still a dirty word in the People's Republic. The fact is that the human rights concept, though enshrined in a self-styled universal declaration, is culture bound. Thus it assumes the rightful supremacy of law and due process over moral teachings; but right-thinking Maoists, who do not tolerate a legal profession, scorn the letter of the law and exalt Mao's principles of moral conduct. They view our civil rights as a form of political affluence associated with the property rights of our economic affluence, not as something China can use. Chinese individuals relate to state and society in a different way.

The difference between Chinese and Americans is perennially fascinating, almost as fascinating as the difference between men

This chapter is based in part on a review of Orville Schell, *In the People's Republic* (New York: Random House, 1977), in the *New York Review of Books*, May 12, 1977, and in part on a review of Schell's *Watch Out for the Foreign Guests!: China Encounters the West* (New York: Pantheon Books, 1981) that appeared as "Drop by Drop" in the *New York Review of Books*, April 16, 1981. Reprinted with permission from the *New York Review of Books*. Copyright © 1977, 1981 Nyrev, Inc.

and women, though less tangible and not as easy to investigate. Whether the Chinese can learn anything moral from us, beyond seeing negative examples in our streets and media, is quite uncertain. Since they have lived crowded longer than we, perhaps we have more to learn from them in both material ecology and personal self-discipline. Buddhism as well as Confucianism taught them that unease and disorder are rooted in human desires, the very things our consumerist advertising and our travel, health, and sex industries try to cultivate. Exciting ourselves as we do in the name of individualism, we have problems that collectivist China hopes to avoid.

Yet our individualist faith is central to our culture, and Americans in China who are not mesmerized by culture shock invariably seek personal intimacies there, hoping to exchange private thoughts, share perspectives, and enjoy a unique experience. To the organizers of China's new order, such conduct is bourgeois, subversive, and dangerously infectious. But just as the Western competition in the 1890s was to see which explorer could get closest to Lhasa before being thrown out of Tibet, so our present-day visitors to the People's Republic compete to see who can have the most intimate heart-to-heart exchange with a Chinese person.

Orville Schell visited China in 1975 in a party of twenty Americans aged eighteen to sixty who not only had a two-week tour of Peking, Yenan, Sian, Mao's birthplace in Hunan, and Shanghai but also spent a fortnight or so working part-time in a Shanghai factory and another period in the fields of the model Tachai Brigade in Shansi. This special opportunity to be with ordinary Chinese, "the masses," was arranged by the trusted Hinton family (of Putney School in Vermont) who have long been a People's Republic of China (PRC) beachhead in the United States. (Bill Hinton's *Fanshen* is the classic account of land reform in the late 1940s.) At age thirty-five Schell was well prepared with Chinese language, historical studies, and two years of reporting from Vietnam and elsewhere.

In the People's Republic is one of the best of the I-saw-China books that have mushroomed since 1972, because Schell mercifully screens out his American colleagues. Instead of recording the considerable happening that this junket must have been, he concentrates on his personal contacts with Chinese and his ensuing reflections. His search for intimate friendship and mutual exchange is frustrating. First, his Chinese acquaintances are uniformly not interested in the United States, which is beyond their ken and certainly beyond their concern. Even worse, they seem genuinely uninterested in the unique assemblage of preferences, self-images, and personal experiences that adorn and identify an American individual. On the contrary, the Chinese are collectivists, seemingly eager to be just like one another, to work together and not separately, to conform and not deviate, and to get their satisfactions from the approval of the group and constituted authority rather than from realizing private ambitions or any form of self-indulgence. This lack of concern for self, this self-realization within the group, not apart from it, is of course not a transient vogue but the product of many centuries of Confucian family collectivism, now redirected to "serve the people."

For Western journalists, those world-weary scions of individual enterprise, this lack of selfishness is hard to take. Schell faults his Hong Kong confreres for defending their impure outside world by magnifying impurities within China—for example, they persist in reporting amateur prostitution in Peking and Shanghai, mainly for foreigners, whereas the really significant thing is the lack of prostitution in China generally. "China's purity seems intolerable to those of us on the outside who live in a state of such permanent compromise and ambiguity . . . we cannot allow the Chinese to become intelligible unless we see them as flawed . . . by greed, lust, selfishness, and self-gratification."

Walking to work from dormitory to factory, Schell falls in with a clear-eyed, handsome girl named Shao-feng. But a man and woman seen alone together in public are usually considered engaged. Finding herself in this one-on-one boy-meets-girl situation, Shao-feng calls to a girlfriend to join them and then is more at ease. Later in the theater she inadvertently sits down next to Schell, who hopes to get further acquainted. But his male Chinese companion at once sees the problem and simply changes seats with him. Schell wonders if the Chinese "have learned to defy the sexual gravity which keeps the bourgeois world so preoccupied and earthbound."

"Americans are forever trying to get the Chinese to say something illuminating on the subject of their personal relations. They will sit at a table full of commune cadres and officials and ask and expect an answer about premarital sex." Schell concludes that Chinese downplaying of sexuality is a "question of values and not repression." He finds "a directness and a matter-of-factness evident in relations between the sexes." But "there is little time and no encouragement for hedonistic activities."

The same abstention applies to national political issues and decisions, which are discussed extensively but always in the past tense, after the issues have been decided. (In the old days the masses took no part in politics; today they are still wary.) Schell remarks that Chinese would rather talk on "past issues that have been resolved than on present issues that are still being struggled over." Live issues still undecided are no-news nontopics. Only dead issues specifically embalmed in the party line can safely be discussed. It is like knowing all the plots of old movies but never seeing a new one unfold in motion. One senses that the inventors of paper, printing, books, and civil service exams learned long ago to wait for the established texts and not pop off orally and prematurely on current events. Schell concludes that "whatever the Chinese talk about most is precisely what they have the greatest trouble doing. The Chinese talk about criticizing authority a great deal . . . They strike me as extremely obedient, almost paralyzed, in the face of authority."

At the Tachai Brigade store Schell meets a fruit-tree specialist, Mr. Huang, who has been "sent down" to work at Tachai—an intelligent and interesting man with whom he enjoys conversing. Schell asks permission and arranges to see Mr. Huang again. That evening he stays home from the movie to write and to sleep. Suddenly the overhead light is on; the cadre in charge tells him that the date with Mr. Huang has been canceled and since Schell is sick he will stay in next day and not go outdoors. Schell realizes that he has been too inquisitive, "seeking individual experiences, not bending totally to the schedule arranged for us."

13

Chiang Ch'ing:
A First Approximation

While many reporters find little individualism, though plenty of personality, among the Chinese masses, Roxane Witke finds both to be flourishing in the woman leader Chiang Ch'ing. Witke got to Peking in July 1972 as a recognized China specialist (out of Stanford, Chicago, and Berkeley, by way of Binghamton) in order to study Chinese feminism. After Chiang Ch'ing suddenly enlisted her services as a female Edgar Snow and gave her sixty hours of self-revealing discourse, Witke faced a problem: translations of the transcripts, after the first one, were in the end not forthcoming, but she had her own copious notes of a week of marathon sessions with Chiang Ch'ing at Canton plus many photographs, and other exchanges in the year after. Chinese officialdom urged her to forget it but she persisted, trying to fashion an intelligible biography and set it in the historical context of the Shanghai stage and film world of the 1930s, of Yenan in the 1940s, and especially of the Cultural Revolution of the 1960s.

Edgar Snow's task in taking down Mao's youthful saga in 1936 was much easier. Witke's account is more diffuse and less definitive. Hers is a big book, handsomely produced with unique photographs, a useful chronology, lists of terms and persons, and research notes. *Comrade Chiang Ch'ing,* published six months after its subject's fall from a decade of power, was given a *Time* cover story. Critics, whether disappointed or enthusiastic, cannot deny its uniqueness, but it will take some time to judge its historical value.

This chapter is from a review of Roxane Witke, *Comrade Chiang Ch'ing* (Boston: Little, Brown, 1977), that appeared as "Mrs. M. and the Masses" in the *New York Review of Books,* May 12, 1977. Reprinted with permission from the *New York Review of Books.* Copyright © 1977 Nyrev, Inc.

First of all, Chiang Ch'ing's story of her career is a political document, self-serving, incomplete, an island of evidence in a broad ocean of secrecy. Imagine a history of the New Deal based on only the *Congressional Record* and the *ex parte* memoirs of Harold Ickes! Chiang Ch'ing's testimony, though partially vetted by Chou En-lai and others, seems strictly personal, not a product of collective judgment on how to characterize the past. The countertestimony of her predecessors as cultural arbiters, the "Four Villains" she purged (Chou Yang, T'ien Han, Hsia Yen, and Yang Han-sheng), of course is not equally available—nor are her statements, direct or indirect, on power relations and leadership decisions either formally authorized by her or fully documented, if at all. The book is not based on tapes as *Khrushchev Remembers* is; it presents Chiang Ch'ing's oral views and recollections as translated by her interpreter, recorded by Roxane Witke in 1972, and subsequently combined with Witke's own research and interpretation. Two voices speak, but it would not be correct to put Chiang Ch'ing's in quotation marks. The author presents her own record of what Chiang Ch'ing said and then her own comment on it. The reader has to shift gears accordingly.

Chiang Ch'ing became an antiparty traitor. Given the secret style of government and the moral obloquy heaped upon former power holders in Peking, this might be expected. But Americans trying in their more open, pluralistic world to penetrate the mystery of Chinese politics can feel indebted to Roxane Witke for her painstaking effort to put Chiang Ch'ing's story together, even though the result is only as reliable as the star witness.

In brief, her early life is presented as one of dire poverty and hardship mixed with determination to rise as an actress and join the revolution. She was accepted by the party in 1933 at age nineteen and, although never an insider in the organization, she worked in the precarious communist underground in Shanghai while becoming known as the actress Li Yun-ho and later as the film star Lan P'ing. She reveals that in 1934 she was jailed for eight months by the Kuomintang (this is now used against her) and released only through the intervention of a foreigner affiliated with the YMCA.

When she reached Yenan with this revolutionary record in August 1937 and took the name Chiang Ch'ing (Azure River), Mao

Tse-tung was forty-four. He took an immediate interest in her, and soon they were married. Her big-city sophistication complemented his country background. At twenty-three she had enough feminist ego to stand up to him and enough resilience to learn his rustic way of life. During the North Shensi campaign of the civil war in 1947–1948 she stayed with Mao and Chou En-lai in villagers' hovels, often marching by night, eluding the Nationalist forces. From this harsh experience her health suffered (tuberculosis, cancer, enlarged liver, and so on). She was ill during most of the 1950s and made four trips to the USSR to recuperate. Only in the late 1950s did she begin to emerge in party councils and campaigns as a leader in her own right.

Chiang Ch'ing finally entered history as an apostle of the Cultural Revolution. After some experience in land reform, she went back to Shanghai in 1959 and began her attack on feudal and bourgeois holdovers in the performing arts there in 1962. "She had convinced the Chairman (as she had argued for years) of the compelling need to gain the upper hand ideologically by vigorously promoting proletarian supremacy in the arts." She felt that China's cultural life, unlike the economy and polity, had not yet been cleansed of its preliberation evils.

Chiang Ch'ing's approach to the cultural superstructure of revolutionary education, art, and literature took off from Mao's formulations and methods for thought reform devised at Yenan in the 1940s. Yet as Witke remarks: "The conflict between totalitarian political authority and creative independence *is* unreconcilable—universally. But in the rhetoric of Mao Tse-tung's regime that insoluble contradiction was grossly oversimplified to supply evidence of the 'struggle between the two lines': the correct line of Mao . . . and the incorrect line of his opponent of the hour." In short, Mao used thought reform politically to show that "people who disagreed with him intellectually were by the same act disloyal to him personally." This approach suited Chiang Ch'ing, who bitterly resented her nonacceptance by the party's cultural commissars of the 1930s. In the 1960s she cashiered them as reactionaries (they had dominated the scene for thirty years) and took their place.

As Mao's greatest campaign unfolded, Chiang Ch'ing drafted key documents, began to reform the Peking opera, and soon made public appearances and even speeches. She became a member of the People's Congress, then cultural adviser to the army, and finally in 1966 one of the Cultural Revolution group appointed to direct the whole campaign. By its end in 1969 she was at the top—a member of the Politburo and in charge of all cultural activities. Including five years of primary school, she had had only eight years of education herself. She let the universities remain closed for five years, stopped all unauthorized book and film production, and sponsored the creation of eight revolutionary operas that blanketed the country with black-and-white stereotypes of villains thwarted by model heroes and heroines, fists clenched in determination, eyes glaring in righteous defiance. This proletarian morality held sway until Mao died in September 1976 and his widow was arrested in October.

Evaluation of Chiang Ch'ing's role in history will depend on one's view of the Cultural Revolution, which had a bad press outside China. Photos showed rampaging teenagers waving their little red books of Mao quotations. To purge the party bureaucrats, Mao mobilized these adolescents as Red Guards, but millions of them later had to be dispersed to the countryside. What did all the chaos accomplish?

Our American incomprehension of Mao's second revolution stems, I think, from our ignorance of China's ancient ruling-class tradition, which was its institutional target. Unfortunately, Mao's quest for the egalitarianism that would bring the masses of China into modern life coincided with the technology of mass communications that foster central control. The revolution's push for equality in social relations and living conditions has not dimmed its need for top authority. The party dictatorship has therefore manipulated the masses even more actively than the old scholar-official elite used to manipulate the *lao-pai-hsing* (or common people) with the skills of Confucian-Legalist statecraft.

Communist elitism is implicit in the whole mystique of the masses to which Chiang Ch'ing subscribed. She felt that to go among the masses, be accepted, win their confidence, and lead them was the revolutionary's highest function. As Mao put it: "Only by being their pupil can he be their teacher. If he regards himself as their master . . . he will not be needed by the masses." Despite this rhetoric, China's politics remain authoritarian. Elitist government of the sophisticated type that has held 800 million Chinese together cannot be soon forgone. From this perspective what outsider can say that Chiang Ch'ing's simplistic operas were not efficacious among China's masses? Her decade of power can be fully judged only in the light of facts we still lack.

For our present purposes one conclusion seems evident—a selected elite committed to governing by egalitarian models and maintaining its established authority over the mass of the populace cannot be expected to embrace a foreign and essentially bourgeois creed of civil liberties. Before we beat the drum of human rights in our China policy, we need to sort out global universals from culture-bound particulars and find common ground. To many Chinese much of our liberty seems closer to license. Let us grant that neither of us can be a model for the other and get down to the business of human survival together.

14

The Succession Crisis of 1976
and the End of the Mao-Chou Era

On January 8, 1976, Prime Minister Chou En-lai died. On April 5 his protégé, the acting prime minister, Deng Xiaoping, was removed from office. On September 9 Mao Tse-tung died, and within two years Deng was in power as China's "paramount leader." What was this all about?

• • •

When Chinese politics mystify us, we should keep in mind that they also mystify even the Chinese close at hand. The fall of acting prime minister Deng Xiaoping must be seen in this light. In the old days the emperor might sack his chief minister overnight and reinstate him the day after, just to show who was boss. The imperial power was arbitrary and uncertain, a constant threat to officeholders. The higher you rose in the hierarchy, the more sudden might be your fall. Chairman Mao as the top man of his day retained this dragonlike quality of unpredictability.

Of course the Chinese political style also mystifies us foreigners simply because we are ignorant. We must learn, for example, that the written word in Chinese characters has had more potency than our alphabetic-phonetic writing. Things put into writing become much more serious than if simply spoken, because the power of the pen, the prestige of learning, adds force to the Chinese written word. The way to start a riot against an unpopular official or an aggressive missionary in the nineteenth century was to post placards in public that called on all right-thinking men to assemble at

Part of this chapter appeared in *Newsday*, March 26, 1976. The remainder is taken from "On the Death of Mao," in the *New York Review of Books*, October 14, 1976. Reprinted with permission from the *New York Review of Books*. Copyright © 1976 Nyrev, Inc.

a given time and place. The rest was easy. The big-character posters and wall newspapers of today are direct descendants of this old custom.

We must try to see the trauma of Mao's death in its Chinese setting. Unfortunately, the esoteric jargon of Chinese politics befuddles as fast as it explains; one must find a middle ground to see China in English-language American terms. First of all, China is still in the shadow of an enormous, overhanging past. Mao was already a young man when the last emperor abdicated in 1912. In July 1976, not many weeks before his death, he must have been impressed by the portent of the terrible Tangshan earthquake—so appropriate to the demise of a Son of Heaven. Mao complained of the Mao cult, but I wonder if he could have avoided it. Having been the One Man for so long, in a spot set apart over two thousand years for someone superhuman, of course he left a fearful hole at the apex of state and society.

China's ten days' mourning reminded us of ours for FDR and JFK—an eerie time when even our commercials stopped; having no commercials, China's network was less disrupted. But to fill out the comparison we should add in our national cult of retrospective grief for Abraham Lincoln. The United States had only four years of the Great Emancipator who saved the union; the Chinese had twenty-seven of their Great Helmsman who brought unity. Few can remember anyone else at the top.

Moreover, the Chinese rely on moral personality and the slow accumulation of personal connections more than on due process to legitimize their leader. Mr. Ford would never have made it in Peking. That he did so in Washington testifies to our constitutional reliance upon legal procedure, which Confucians and Maoists alike have regarded askance as inhibiting true morality. China is thus more vulnerable and insecure than we are during a change of leaders. Sons of Heaven were removed only by death. So with Prime Minister Chou and Chairman Mao.

But why was Deng Xiaoping attacked? Answers come at several levels. The first is that he had lost his protector, Chou En-lai, who had resuscitated Deng from the disgrace meted out to him in the Cultural Revolution almost a decade earlier. The death of Chou En-lai on January 8 was a great loss to both China and ourselves. Chou was the chief executive who had handled decisions at the top of the government for twenty-five years. He was also the moving spirit in China's foreign relations, who in his youth had visited Japan and been a student in France, whereas Mao had never left home. Chou was the negotiator abroad who traveled widely in Europe, Asia, and Africa to represent the People's Republic. With this wider perspective he was also the chief conciliator, who patched up quarrels and kept to the middle ground under Mao's leadership.

For forty years the linchpin of the Mao-Chou relationship was Chou's loyalty to Mao as leader. Except in the field of foreign relations, where Chou built up the foreign ministry and ambassadorial staffs, he avoided the creation of a clique or faction within the party. For twenty years Liu Shao-ch'i remained second to Mao Tse-tung as leader of the party establishment, more experienced in proletarian organization in the cities and among transport workers, while Mao went among the peasantry. When Liu was eliminated in the Cultural Revolution of the late 1960s, his place as Number Two was taken by the army leader Lin Piao, who then died mysteriously in an alleged plot to assassinate Mao.

Meanwhile Chou remained safely in the Number Three position with no hint of rivalry with the leader for power. However, after Chou became ill with cancer in 1973, Deng Xiaoping soon moved into his place as acting premier.

That Deng should come under attack from the radical true believers who saw Mao as their patron and who rose to prominence in the Cultural Revolution was not illogical. The Chinese Revolution under Mao was energized by the dynamic tension between the themes of moral regeneration and technological development, of "red" and "expert." This is a dualism that has had a long tradition in Chinese politics. The ancient Confucian faith was that man is rational and that his conduct can be improved by teaching, exhortation, and study of classical models. Consequently, Confucian reformers were constantly arising to denounce backsliding among bureaucrats and even to admonish the emperor. Quoting the classics, they could be superrighteous and terrorize officeholders, much like American patrioteers who wrap themselves in the flag and denounce proforeign or communistic tendencies.

Come the revolution, this ideological superrighteousness has had a field day in China. On the one hand, today's bureaucrats, as inheritors of the world's oldest bureaucratic tradition, have organized party and government to accomplish modern tasks, maximize production, and lift China out of weakness and poverty. Yet on the other hand, the theme of moral regeneration is the essence of the revolution, and Mao stood on the side of continual revolutionary effort to remake Chinese thinking and values at the same time that he presided over the whole movement. The Cultural Revolution was his distinct creation, and Deng as party secretary-general became its Number Two target. Only with mixed feelings did Mao see him brought back to power in 1973.

On a deeper level, American observers must never forget (as we all do) that China is still primarily a land of farmers who used to be peasants, and therefore out of politics; that the old ruling class used to run things as a small, literate, highly qualified elite, and that this is one of China's strongest traditions. After all, the T'ang court institutionalized the examination system hundreds of years before the Western Europeans had printed books to read or even governments to seek qualified officials. This means that the slogan "Serve the people," the heart of Mao's revolutionary idea, required building up the countryside, where the people still live. Building up the state and its central industrial power was a different, more conventional, and to us more understandable goal. But if pursued at all costs, it could smother the revolution. Therefore, Mao remained center-left and gave the radicals, who dominated the media, their chance to attack Deng as an establishment figure.

Against this background what are we to make of the poster and press attacks on Deng, who was supplanted by another acting premier but retained his basic posts in the party and at the top of the Military Affairs Commission? One way to look at it is to note that in 1976 both the American and the Chinese people were in the throes of a succession crisis. We met it by voting in thirty primaries, two party conventions, and a national election in a process that occupied a year. The Chinese met it in a different way, and since Mao was the founding father of the revolution, they faced a larger crisis than we did. No doubt the death of Chou En-lai before Mao weakened Mao's performance. Would Nixon have been invited to visit Peking a second time (after Watergate) if Chou had still been prime minister? The Chinese intent behind Nixon's second coming was plainly to reaffirm the rapprochement between Peking and

Washington that he had inaugurated, and by implication to suggest that his successor had been slow to carry out the American part of the Shanghai communique of February 1972.

Undoubtedly this message got across. But it involved Chairman Mao in seeming to support and condone the conduct of a disgraced president who left office because of high crimes and misdemeanors against our Constitution. One can only conclude that Chairman Mao was peculiarly insensitive to these principles. In brief, Mr. Nixon offended against the American secular faith in due process and individual rights. In American terms he was an impious figure. But Mao Tse-tung was seldom concerned with individual rights or due process. Perhaps he justified the invitation on the basis that "my enemy's enemy is my friend," but it was not a way to enhance his stature in American eyes.

The fact that without Chou En-lai handling China's foreign relations, Chairman Mao marched to a different drummer would not have been so upsetting if only we could have heard the beat of social revolution more clearly. Peking's policy issues have inhered in the distinction between the industrial revolution and the social revolution. The industrial revolution of modern times, as applied to China, has increased production in both industry and agriculture through new technology, literacy, public health, capital investment, and new forms of organization. This is the province of those we label "pragmatists" or "moderates," whom we like to think we understand and can even identify with. (Actually they are sincere enemies of free enterprise and individualism.) The social revolution in China has been *sui generis*, quite beyond our experience, a struggle against China's most persistent heritage, the ruling-class tradition. This heritage included the Confucian teachings of social order based on the natural inequality of status between elders and youth, men and women, rulers and ruled. The tradition was highly elitist. The small ruling class produced China's remarkable literature and philosophy, patronized her arts and commerce, and ran her affairs both local and imperial while living off the peasantry.

The attack on China's outworn social structure was Mao's province from the beginning, after his heterodox report of 1927 on the peasantry as the real vanguard of revolution. "Liberation" during the Yenan decade from 1936 to 1946 brought the peasant a sense of freedom, literacy, and some technology. But primarily Yenan trained new party cadres to mobilize the peasantry for production, war, and politics. After 1949 the great mass organizations and national campaigns retrained the bureaucrats and scholars, and gradually eliminated both landlords and capitalists.

But Mao found to his dismay that it was not enough to eliminate the old ruling-class leftovers. The elitist virus was encysted within the body politic. The revolution's newly liberated peasants were not only incipient capitalists, European fashion, they also had it in their bones to rise in the social scale and make a new ruling class. Special privilege reappeared in the Communist Party apparatus, sprouting from the deep soil of China's tradition. In the Cultural Revolution of 1966–1969, Mao tried to root it out. How especially Chinese this problem is, how exotic to America, was evidenced in May Seventh schools, where white-collar city workers from librarians to commissars regularly got their hands dirty farming like peasants. "Class struggle" thus has a special meaning in Chinese social history. "Serve the people" means no more upper-class privilege.

Yet this supremely Maoist slogan makes plain the problem it seeks to overcome. Chinese officialdom, now so extraordinarily swollen in size, is heir to its own tradition of avowedly benevolent manipulation of the masses. In updating this upper-class responsibility to "bring order to the empire," Mao as sage and teacher led in a process of tutelage, bringing the masses into political life, setting them upon the road of self-reliant development. The need for tutelage, for nurturing of self-government among a politically inert though often rebellious peasantry, was obvious to reformers like Liang Ch'i-ch'ao at the start of the century. Sun Yat-sen made tutelage central to his program. Mao put it in other terms, but his would-be egalitarian order is still managed by an elite party. Travelers in the People's Republic are struck by the strong sense of hierarchy still remaining as a necessary component of social order and by the party cadres' sense of duty to "serve the people" as a special calling.

To summarize, Mao's revolution for the people could not be led originally by the people. Democratic participation had to be organized and distributed to them. Mao was the Great Distributor—of peasant rights, women's emancipation, public welfare, scientific technology, self-respect, national pride. But distribution had its price. In filling up the valleys it tore down the peaks. The effort to change the character of the people has imposed orthodoxy and conformity, limitation of knowledge, suppression of individuality. Intellectuals were starved for books and cowed by doctrinaire organizers. Higher education was suspended for five years outright and has been revived mainly as technical training. But some Chinese distributionists argue that even higher technology can be imported when needed. They see no need for "pure science," only for "applied."

In a curious way that has been little studied, the protagonists of moral principle (redness) over material technology (expertness) are reminiscent of nineteenth-century scholar-officials who decried Western material inventions and espoused the imperial Confucian tradition of government by men of rectitude and virtue. Those impassioned conservatives wrapped themselves in Confucian righteousness and obstructed China's modernization for a whole generation. I am not suggesting a lineal descent from them to Mao (Chiang Ch'ing was no Empress Dowager), but merely a resonance of style. Militant denunciation by standards of absolute morality is an old Chinese as well as Maoist custom. There is more history behind politburo diatribes than is visible to the gimlet-eyed astigmatism of American political science.

Peking's policy struggle has echoes of Peking's past at the same time that it arises over hard practical choices—how far to continue Mao's crusade against the elitism and special privilege of the past, how far to stress a necessarily elitist buildup of modern technology and expertise. "Red versus expert," moral-political qualities versus technical-productive abilities, will continue to be an issue. There are many other issues that outsiders can only dimly perceive through the veil of secrecy.

One is the issue of secrecy itself. How long can the Central Committee act like a palace guard immune to scrutiny? How long can the world press be treated as spies and reduced (or elevated?) to the Chinese practice of studying obscure poetic references and indirect historical allusions in order to understand policy? Probably this can go on for a long time. After Anglo-French gunfire in 1860 secured the right of Western diplomats to stay in Peking, it was another seventeen years before Chinese diplomats were stationed in European capitals. We cannot judge China by ourselves. But we try every day.

How to evaluate Mao Tse-tung will inspire a large literature among us. He was not a small man. Look at his treatment of the United States. Nineteenth-century and early twentieth-century Americans in China did much to stir up the great revolution, but when it came to power in 1949 we opposed it. We fought the Chinese quite unnecessarily in Korea: after MacArthur landed at Inchon and before he went for the Yalu to conquer North Korea, Chou En-lai explained to us that China could not let a friendly buffer state be supplanted by an avowed enemy on the border of her Manchurian industrial base. In Korea we caused a million Chinese casualties. We later compounded this by bombing North Vietnam with many invasions of Chinese air space, a humiliation to all patriots. But Mao stayed out, and in the end—because we had become less of a problem than the Russians—he invited the leader of our defeat to visit Peking. Plainly he would sup with the devil for *raisons d'état*.

With help from Chou En-lai and some millions of others, Mao led the People's Republic through a phase of history that has now come to an end. Will we be able to achieve any fuller comprehension of China's problems now that he and his generation are gone? The new generation will be equally absorbed in domestic issues, as usual in China, and we shall have to understand them largely by our own efforts, through barriers of language and ideology. Mao-and-Chou were a brilliant team, and we shall need to emulate their foresight, patience, and tenacity if we are to maintain normal relations by recognizing Peking's sovereignty over Taiwan while also ensuring the stability and autonomy of Taiwan.

But we have wasted the generation of opportunity afforded us in the aftermath of our period of activity in China up to 1949. The Chinese revolutionary leadership, when it came to power, had already had extensive contact with Americans and American ways. Chou En-lai had negotiated with General Marshall. Chou's director of information had attended a Shanghai missionary school; her sister had worked with Mrs. Roosevelt. China's first envoy to the United Nations was a graduate of Tsing Hua, the university supported by Boxer indemnity funds that America returned to China. His successor at the United Nations had attended Yenching University, the leading American missionary college. Edgar Snow was Mao's biographer. More Americans than Russians had got to Yenan when the People's Republic was in gestation there. The catalogue could go on and on.

Precisely because the American influence was so strong in China before 1949, the communist revolution felt compelled to wipe it out, just as the Americans felt the "loss of China" as a result. But in the contradictory dialectical way so characteristic of Mao's thought, the Americans, though on the wrong side in Chinese history, were nevertheless a known quantity with whom relations could be resumed—as they have been.

Now the generation that knew us has departed. The many American-trained Chinese professors and scientists are either dead or retired or close to it. In the years of estrangement since the failure of General Marshall's mediation in 1946, those who made the great revolution, and who knew Americans as onetime allies against Japan, have trained a new generation, who know Americans only as copybook capitalist-imperialists, the defeated bombers of Vietnam. The heritage of positive Sino-American relations before 1949 has been dissipated, not used when it might have been used to help achieve more constructive contact with Peking. The end of the Mao-and-Chou era has not eased our way toward peace and progress in Chinese-American relations.

PART THREE

The Road to Normalization

The American image of China began to shift as the embattled cold-war spirit of opposing "communism" in all its forms at all times everywhere gave way to a more discriminating American view of the outer world.

First, the Sino-Soviet split was the big new international fact of the 1960s. It would lead by 1970 to the idea of a triangular relationship between Washington, Moscow, and Peking. In retrospect, it is amazing how long it took us to recognize national communism when we saw it emerge in both China and North Vietnam. So powerful was our fixation on the Absolute Evil of "communism" that we could not believe it would suffer from international power politics within Moscow's worldwide conspiracy. We blindly and stubbornly disregarded the surfacing in 1960 of the Sino-Soviet rift. Khrushchev could suddenly yank the thousands of Soviet engineers and advisers out of China together with their blueprints, and true communist believers around the world could feel their universe tottering, but noncommunist Americans could only wonder what kind of new stratagem "the communists" were trying to fool us with. Witness the fact that we went into Vietnam *after* 1960, while Moscow and Peking were already publicly denouncing each other. Our ostensible reason was to rescue South Vietnam from Moscow's worldwide tentacles. For eight years we tried to stop the brutal North Vietnamese unification of Vietnam, largely in order to keep Communist China from expanding its power southward, only to find by 1979 that China and Vietnam had become first-class enemies with daggers drawn. This perspective makes our Vietnam venture of the 1960s seem all the more stupid.

Next, we had to realize—haltingly and often unwillingly—that China under Mao, contrary to our cold-war rhetoric, had not actually been expansive beyond China's old Inner Asian realm. It took us a long time to conclude this from the evidence of the Sino-Indian border war of 1962.

Finally, it became apparent that Mao's strident turning inward in the 1960s had not paid off in revolutionary success and that China would have to turn outward again by enlarging foreign contact. This meant a resumption of Sino-American relations that presupposed a change in Taiwan-American relations. Nixon in Peking in 1972 brought to a focus the long-dormant issue of the American alliance with Taiwan. A solution began to emerge in the acceptance of the One China myth of the Chinese state, coupled with the continued self-government of the province of Taiwan. The "one-country, two-systems" stance of 1984 was already foreshadowed.

15

Reappraisal of Chinese Aggressiveness: The 1962 Border War with India

Peking's "expansionism" had been the major justification for the United States' containment policy. The sudden Chinese attack on Indian border forces in October 1962 was denounced by India as unprovoked aggression, and it contributed to the American image of a China that was "expansionist." This pillar of the containment doctrine has been carefully examined by Neville Maxwell, who breaks it up and throws it to the winds as an object lesson in international astigmatism—primarily that of the Indians, but also ours. His story tells us something about the Chinese style in boundary disputes, if not in foreign relations generally, and raises questions to ponder as we look at the Sino-American future and the question of Taiwan in particular.

Neville Maxwell is an Australian educated at McGill and at Cambridge universities, who spent three years in the Washington bureau of the London *Times* and then in 1959 went to New Delhi as the *Times*'s South Asia correspondent. There he reported on the Sino-Indian border dispute as well as on the last years of the Nehru government. After eight years in and around India, he went to London to research this book at the School of Oriental and African Studies. As he says, no recent international quarrel has been "so fully documented and . . . so widely and totally misunderstood." He follows in the footsteps of Alastair Lamb (author of *The China-India Border: The Origins of the Disputed Boundaries* and *The McMahon Line: A Study in the Relations between India, China,*

This review of Neville Maxwell, *India's China War* (London: J. Cape, 1970; New York: Pantheon Books, 1971), appeared as "How Aggressive Is China?" in the *New York Review of Books,* April 22, 1971. Reprinted with permission from the *New York Review of Books.* Copyright © 1971 Nyrev, Inc.

and Tibet, 1904–1914) and other British researchers, and his full, meticulous documentation is informed not only by his own experience on the scene but also by confidential sources on the Indian side.

Even without Maxwell's having any inside view from Peking, the Chinese performance in this dispute as shown in the Indian record begins quite early to shine forth as both rational and reasonable, while the Indian performance grows steadily more irrational and unreasonable. The tone is illustrated by Nehru's oft-repeated statements that (1) in the cause of peace he would talk to anyone, anywhere, at any time, and (2) over India's sacred boundaries he would absolutely never negotiate. Nehru's distinction between "talks" and "negotiations" enabled him to appeal to the world while avoiding any settlement with China.

The Sino-Indian boundary offered a fine opportunity for statesmanship, involving far less flammable issues than the Taiwan question does today. For more than two thousand years the Chinese and Indian peoples had developed their great civilizations on either side of the Himalayan massif with an absolute minimum of contact. But the Chinese and Indian republics, when they got rid of their imperial rulers, immediately claimed the imperial boundaries that their late rulers had built up.

Thus the Chinese Republic after 1911, having ended the Manchu dynasty, at once laid claim to all territories the Manchus had conquered, including Outer Mongolia and Tibet. Chiang Kai-shek always had the same idea, but the Chinese were not strong enough to make good these claims in Tibet until 1950, and they are still frustrated over Outer Mongolia by the Russian support of its independence. But British India never succeeded in making Tibet a protectorate, acknowledged by the outer world as a sovereign state, and when the People's Republic began calling it "the Tibet region of China," there was no basis in international law for objecting to it.

The boundary disputes arose at the eastern and western ends of the frontier. At the eastern end, the McMahon Line, later so famous, was really never anything but a line drawn by Captain Henry McMahon in 1914, to which no Chinese government had ever agreed. It followed the crest of the ridge of mountains on the edge of the Tibetan plateau some 140 miles north of the plains of Assam. In the decade before their departure, the British revived it as a claim line and moved posts into the disputed area south of the McMahon Line. India inherited this occupied territory.

Meanwhile the western end of the Sino-Indian boundary remained even more uncertain, both undefined and undelimited. Various British proconsuls had suggested three different alignments, for which there were eleven different variations in the record. Following a directive of Nehru in 1954, India claimed the most extreme of these British proposals of earlier days, one that would reach beyond the Karakoram to the K'un Lun range and would include within India, the Aksai Chin, or "desert of white stone," although no Indian patrol had ever gone that far north. Then India found that in 1956–1957 the Chinese had built a 750-mile motor road from Yarkand across Aksai Chin to Gartok, connecting Tibet to Sinkiang. Tibetan and Central Asian traders had long used this route, and it was the only feasible one for motor contact. No Indian people or government representatives were anywhere in the region, and India made a formal claim to it only in 1958.

With all these claims still unresolved but in the background, the early 1950s saw a Chinese-Indian love affair based on the theme of *"Hindee Chinee bhai-bhai"* (India-China brotherhood) and on the famous five principles of peaceful coexistence. Nehru was being a world statesman on the basis of nonalignment, and India was felt to be competing with Communist China to lead the development of Asia. Neither country's welfare or progress was dependent on their mutual boundary line in the godforsaken wastes of the high Himalaya and K'un Lun ranges. A more thoroughly unimportant issue can hardly be imagined, except that it became a focus of patriotic concern to Nehru and then to all India. Once the issue was raised, the essential strategic point was that, owing to the more gradual slope on the north, China had roads up to its claim lines, whereas India, approaching the Himalayan escarpment from the south, had no vehicular access to its claim lines.

"By 1958," as Maxwell puts it, "the two no-man's-lands which the imperial era had left at opposite ends of the Sino-Indian frontier had thus been occupied, each side pre-empting the area which was important to it on strategic and practical considerations." The Chinese took the position that both boundaries were in dispute, had never been delimited, and therefore should be negotiated. As a general proposal, China would accept the hitherto unacceptable McMahon Line because the Indians had now moved up to it, and China would ask India to accept the Chinese possession of Aksai Chin in the same spirit. This remained the Chinese position throughout the controversy. There was little nonsense about the sacred soil of the motherland—after all, no Chinese had ever lived in the Assam Himalayas or on the Karakoram range, there were no great strategic problems, and the main issue should be mutual expediency.

On the Indian side, however, it was not so simple. The Chinese takeover of Tibet and the suppression of Tibetan rebels, the flight of the Dalai Lama in 1959 to political asylum in India, and then the charges of Chinese genocide in Tibet, all heated up the New Delhi atmosphere. To Chou En-lai's proposal to negotiate, Nehru replied that India's boundaries were already clear and established and could never be negotiated. Chou En-lai had suggested that pending a negotiated delimitation the status quo should be accepted in both disputed areas, but Nehru with semantic slipperiness agreed to the "status quo" in the sense that China should return to her position before she had built the Aksai Chin road and withdraw from all territory claimed by India. Thus Nehru's "status quo" meant really "status quo ante."

Nehru was of course up against the Opposition in New Delhi, and its increasing jingoism led him into a rhetorical escalation. Soon he was saying that the Indian claim lines found in the half-forgotten and uneffectuated nineteenth-century proposals of British proconsuls had "always been the historic frontiers" of India, and were "not open to discussion with anybody." China was really asking for the Himalayas, which were "the crown of India," part of her "culture, blood and veins." China was acting with "the pride and arrogance of might . . . just to show us our place . . . so that we may not get uppish." China was trying to bully India. To negotiate with China would be backing down.

Pretty soon Nehru went further and declared that the boundary had in fact already been delimited. The boundary had been "approximately where it now runs for nearly three thousand years."

This soaring rhetoric was not without tergiversation. In August and September 1959 Nehru said that no clear boundary had ever been defined in the western sector. But by November he declared that "any person with a knowledge of history . . . would appreciate that this traditional and historical frontier of India has been associated with India's culture and tradition for the last two thousand years and has been an intimate part of India's life and thought."

The effect of this flood of words was to befuddle the outside world with the view that China was indeed being aggressive, as the West already assumed. But its worst effect was to befuddle the prime minister himself. He had now denounced China's presence in Aksai Chin as aggression and so found he had to do something about it. The result was his "forward policy," by which Indian army patrols were to be sent into the Chinese-occupied Aksai Chin area from the beginning of 1960 to establish an Indian presence there and undermine the Chinese position. Maxwell points out a curious similarity: the forward policy would in effect apply to the Chinese the same tactics of *satyagraha* that the Indians had used against the British. Instead of passive civil disobedience, however, this policy would now be implemented by armed troops, whose presence would oblige the Chinese to give way, for if they used force it would rebound against them just as it had against the British in India.

To the professional generals of the Indian army, the forward policy seemed like dangerous nonsense. At both the western and the eastern ends of the disputed Sino-Indian boundary, the Chinese had feeder roads that brought truck supplies and reinforcements to their border posts. The Indian army, on the contrary, had no roads anywhere near the forward positions it was now asked to assume. All supplies, even sometimes water, had to come by air-drop. Troops patrolling at fourteen or fifteen thousand feet had to be acclimatized, but they frequently lacked arctic clothing; Indian patrols went forward with only the ammunition and blankets they could carry on their backs.

In the face of these logistic and climatic obstacles, the Indian army held back until late in 1961. The forward policy was not really put into effect until the Nehru administration put political generals into the high command. These were inexperienced careerists who were ready to do the civilians' bidding partly because they were themselves militarily incompetent and knew no better. Such politicization of the Indian high command injected into the developing debacle an element not only of incompetence but of downright imbecility.

The eventual disaster was precipitated in 1962 by the carrying-out of the Indian forward policy. Posts were set up on the Indian claim lines so that the armed forces of the two sides were within range in fluid situations concerning which India still refused to negotiate. Chou En-lai reiterated his proposals for negotiated delimitation of boundaries and, pending that, for mutual withdrawals, twenty kilometers on each side, until the diplomats could work out a settlement. All this was refused by the Nehru government, which asserted that its unilateral claims were nonnegotiable, while meantime claiming to the world that the Indian patrols were defending themselves against Chinese aggression. Border firefights began to occur, but the Chinese held back from using their superior equipment.

The Indian political generals were urged on by the Indian politicians who assured them that the Chinese would never retaliate and would withdraw under pressure. "The press and governments of the Western world cheered India on, as they saw her pluckily standing her ground against what they believed to be the expansionist drive of China."

By August 1962 there were some forty Indian posts, each comprising a dozen or twoscore troops, within the Chinese claim lines under the guns of the adjoining Chinese outposts. Supplied by air only, they were quite helpless, "hostages to the conviction of Nehru and his associates in New Delhi, civilian and military, that China would never attack." But this reckless Indian gamble to threaten to expel the Chinese by force instead of negotiation was represented by Nehru as being purely defensive, and consequently he was under attack in New Delhi for possible appeasement. He had painted himself into a corner.

The border war was triggered when the Indians sent twenty-five hundred troops, in summer uniforms and with only the equipment they could carry, across high passes north of the McMahon Line, with orders to assault Chinese bunkers that were heavily reinforced on the mountain ridges farther north. This truly suicidal project was denounced by some of the professional officers, who resigned on the spot, but was ordered by the political generals now in command. Supplying a post at 15,500 feet, for example, required a five-day climb by porters from the air strip, and on a ten-day round trip the porters could carry almost no payloads beyond what they needed for their own survival. Among twenty-five hundred troops beyond the McMahon Line only two or three hundred had winter clothing and tents, and none had axes or digging tools, to say nothing of heavy guns or adequate ammunition. As ordered, they mounted a small attack, and the Chinese reacted and drove it back on October 10.

The Chinese reaction to the announced Indian buildup for an attack north of the McMahon Line initially produced in New Delhi not only the excitement of warfare but even euphoria. Chou En-lai's proposal that everybody stop where they were and negotiate was again denounced as aggressive. Nehru said that China's proposal "would mean mere existence at the mercy of an aggressive, arrogant and expansionist neighbor." He began to accept American and British military aid as well as Russian. As Maxwell remarks, "It was almost forgotten that the Indian army had been about to take offensive action; ignored, that the government had refused to meet the Chinese for talks." Meanwhile, after their initial reaction, the Chinese paused and built roads to supply their advanced positions, while the Indian forces were kept widely distributed in defenseless, small contingents, still in the belief that the Chinese would never dare to attack.

All this was resolved on November 17, when the Chinese did attack again and in three days overran or routed all the ill-supplied Indian forces in the field, east and west. Many brave Indian troops died at their posts and were found frozen there months later. India's political generals behaved like headless chickens. The Indian defeat was complete. On November 21, 1962, China announced a unilateral cease-fire and a withdrawal in the west by stages to positions twenty kilometers behind their lines of control and in the east to the north of the McMahon Line, so that they would hold essentially what they had been proposing for three years past.

But the Indian government, while accepting the cease-fire in fact, objected to the proposal publicly. Its forward policy was finished and two or three thousand Indian troops had been lost; but "no negotiations" was still the Indian policy. "The border war, almost universally reported as an unprovoked Chinese invasion of India, had only confirmed the general impression that Peking pursued a reckless, chauvinistic and belligerent foreign policy." China had won the match, but India the verdict.

Neville Maxwell's picture of Indian ineptitude was the end product of much study by many observers, both Indian and foreign. His picture of Chinese reasonableness in this case seems unlikely to be greatly altered by new information in the future. But Chinese negotiators have a wide repertoire of styles. Chou En-lai's readiness to bargain the McMahon Line for the Aksai Chin road contrasted markedly with the intransigent and vituperative behavior of the Chinese military at the Panmunjom bargaining table in Korea, and it said nothing about Peking's feeling about Taiwan, which the People's Republic has always claimed to be even more Chinese than Tibet.

When we seek perspective from this case study on our own dispute with Peking, we see at once that the Sino-Indian frontier and the Sino-American frontier are in opposite circumstances. The Chinese were established in force on their claim lines along the boundary with India. When a reasonable settlement could not be negotiated, they defended their positions with superior power, but did not expand them. In the Formosa strait, on the other hand, Chinese power was inadequate to face the Seventh Fleet, and the Chinese claim to Taiwan could not be made good by force. We may therefore expect it to be preserved in the record in forceful terms, even though an imperfect situation has to be acknowledged, and denounced, in the meantime.

Taiwan as a boundary dispute must be analyzed on two different planes. The first is procedural and de jure: how was a settlement to be reached on the new grounds that "China had stood up," and was now master of her own house and sovereign over Taiwan? Our support of Taiwan's separation from the mainland was in Peking's view a holdover from the imperialist era; and we acknowledged this when we remarked that Taiwan had been separate from the mainland for more than seventy-five years, from 1895 to 1945 under the Japanese empire, and after 1950 under our naval protection.

Liquidation of the old imperialism is therefore one tenet in Peking, and we may note that Peking demanded that the McMahon Line and the Sino-Burmese border, both inherited from the British empire, should be renegotiated in order to purge them of imperialism—although in the end the Sino-Burmese treaty of 1960 and the Sino-Indian Border War of 1962 resulted in China's accepting the lines originally negotiated or proposed by the British. The equivalent in the case of Taiwan would presumably be the universal acknowledgment of Chinese sovereignty over it in de jure form, as demanded by both Peking and Taipei. Pro forma, they still disputed who ruled all China, while both claimed that Taiwan was part of China.

A second plane is that of de facto power relations, and here it is clear that Taiwan as an island was and had been politically independent of the mainland for most of three generations, and was likely to remain so for a long time in the future. This is because Taiwan had become a focus of several interests, in addition to the interest of Peking. These other interests included that of the Taiwanese Chinese population. They were more than 11 million out of the 14 million total and thus they far outnumbered the mainlander element who still controlled the government of the Republic of China. The American public and other peoples around the world were likely to sympathize with the Taiwan Chinese demand for self-determination. Both Japan and the United States meanwhile had a strategic-economic interest, and it was predictable that this Japanese interest would grow stronger with time, while possibly ours might relatively decline.

If Taiwan's separateness from mainland China was thus likely to continue for some time in fact, how could this situation and the idea of self-determination be reconciled with the claims of Chinese sovereignty? The answer, if there was any, lay in the concept of autonomy (*tzu-chih*), a term that in the Chinese lexicon can cover a wide spectrum of situations with varying degrees of central control over the autonomous area in question.

China's performance in the Indian boundary dispute more than two decades ago suggests that the formal de jure situation requires our attention quite as much as the de facto situation, but that the concern for substance, of negotiators of the caliber of Chou En-lai, was likely to be flexible: for example, the imperialist-sponsored McMahon Line could be accepted as part of a bargain when it was

16

Mao's Shift Outward and Nixon's First Trip to Peking

Historians will conclude that our contact with Peking was less surprising than the fact that it was so long delayed. From 1950 to 1971 Washington sent more men to the moon than to China, even though China is closer and more populous, and the trip less costly and dangerous. So deep was the rut of nonrecognition that President Nixon made headlines by uttering the two words "People's Republic." After these magic words, however, a boy from Santa Monica with shoulder-length hair and purple bell-bottom trousers could suddenly find himself in Peking asking the fabulous Chou En-lai, "What do you think of hippies?"

Few lineups in power politics can last beyond a generation, and a Sino-American thaw had been in the cards ever since the Sino-Soviet split of 1960. Rulers of China have been trained by two thousand years of often bitter experience to play off one powerful outsider against another, and generations of Chinese schoolboys have studied the maneuvers of the Three Kingdoms of the third century A.D., much as schoolboys in the expansive West used to be raised on Caesar's conquest of Gaul.

• • •

The Peking of 1971 was in two great-power triangles in which we also figured. With the Soviet Union and the United States, Communist China was a nuclear power, and the Sino-Soviet tensions needed to be balanced by greater American contact. With the

---

Part of this chapter appeared as "The Time is Ripe for China to Shift Outward Again" in the *New York Times*, April 18, 1971. Copyright © 1971 by the New York Times Company. Reprinted by permission. The other portion of the chapter appeared as "It's an Old Chinese Custom: Peking Has Received Potentates for a Thousand Years" in the *Washington Post*, July 19, 1971.

United States and Japan, China was a Western Pacific power concerned about the status of Taiwan, the oil resources on the continental shelf just north of Taiwan, Japan's trade and armament, and similar issues that also concerned Japan and the United States.

All these issues impelled Peking toward playing a greater role abroad, accepting American contact and admission into the United Nations. But Peking had reached this point only after bitter experience with alternatives.

The 1950s saw Communist China's development under the protection of the Sino-Soviet alliance. As Maoism became more plainly nationalistic and romantic and attempted instant industrialization through the Great Leap of 1958, the alliance began to crack.

As the Sino-Soviet split widened into harsh polemics, Peking in the early 1960s sought to go it alone and capture the leadership of the communist world revolution. China exported cultural missions, exhibitions, and military propaganda together with aid, arms, and advice to new nations in support of national "liberation" movements, especially in Asia and Africa.

Mao Tse-tung's effort to range the amorphous Third World against the two superpower blocs was formulated by his heir apparent, Lin Piao, in his September 1965 speech "On People's Wars of Liberation." Expanding China's experience to the world scene, Marshal Lin pictured the Chinese model of revolution as applicable to the underdeveloped two-thirds of mankind in a struggle against the industrialized imperialist powers.

The metaphor was to "surround the cities from the countryside," but there were no printed instructions on how to do this concretely across the world's oceans and continents. The Chinese line advocated self-reliance for all people's revolutions, which meant that China could point the way and offer aid, but not herself achieve the world revolution. This was not a Hitlerite blueprint for conquest abroad, but instead reminded one of the ancient theory of tributary relationships of neighboring states to Peking—the theory that China was a model that other countries should follow, but on their own initiative.

This do-it-yourself prescription for other people's revolutions was issued at a time of setback in Peking's foreign relations. In February 1965 the United States had begun continuous bombing of North Vietnam, and although this aggression on China's doorstep was accompanied by promises not to invade North Vietnam on the ground, the People's Republic in effect had to swallow the humiliation of impotence, unable to protect a traditionally satellite nation next door.

Farther afield, the Chinese effort to organize an Afro-Asian conference excluding the Soviet Union had failed ignominiously in June 1965 and subsequently, in October, an abortive Communist coup in Indonesia was followed by the slaughter of the pro-Peking Indonesian Communists there. In short, 1965 was the year of failure in China's attempted leadership of world revolution, all of which contributed to a turning inward and the subsequent absorption of Chinese attention in Chairman Mao's Great Proletarian Cultural Revolution from 1966 to 1969.

The frenzied excitement of the Cultural Revolution years of political revivalism finally ended with more whimper than bang in an apparent stalemate. Mr. Mao had shaken up the bureaucracy, revived the spirit of revolution, and brought new blood into politics, but the final stabilizing influence proved to be the army officers who were brought into administration all over the country. The Ninth Party Congress of April 1969 finally confirmed the stalemate, and China could concentrate again on economic construction, and also send her ambassadors, most of whom had been called home, back to their posts abroad.

Peking's reentry into world politics was thus a rebound from alternative efforts, first to lead the Third World alone and then to opt out of foreign relations for a time. We have no reason to think that Peking's orchestration of people's diplomacy will omit the usual subversive programs and hard-line bargaining. The apparent readiness of most Americans to get out of Vietnam, coupled with the Nixon administration's long continued overtures toward contact with Peking, indicated that the time was ripe for China to shift outward again. It did so with the Nixon visit.

Among all the other angles, the Nixon trip to Peking in February 1972 needs to be viewed historically from the Chinese end. Visits of heads of state are an old Chinese custom. Peking has been a capital city for roughly a thousand years, and foreign potentates or their envoys have turned up practically every year, as regularly as the winter solstice or the fall equinox. They have come for a variety of motives, most to present tribute in order to profit from trade, some to have their legitimacy confirmed, others to ask for military help, and not a few to demand payoffs to keep them quiet.

Some chiefs of state have come unwillingly, like the King of Malacca in the early 1400s, but some came as conquerors like Genghis Khan in 1215 or the Manchu regent Dorgon in 1644. But in nearly every case the trip to Peking was a memorable event shot through with a special flavor, a certain mystique. Mr. Nixon and his staff, without knowing it, trod well-worn paths.

No one would ask him to perform the three kneelings and nine prostrations of the kowtow, which Lord Macartney refused to perform in 1793 (although Mr. Nixon, unlike Macartney, has the trim figure suited to it). The Maoist revolution has tried to wipe out the ancient unmodern customs. Nevertheless, sinocentrism, the proud consciousness of China's vast self-sufficient magnificence, is not so easily expunged, and part of the charm of going there still lies in the fact that Peking is the center of a different world not concerned about the Dow Jones average, the hemline, the World Series, or the next election. No one can stay for long without feeling reoriented—or rather, oriented—called upon to respond to a different part of the globe and accept the values of a different (for example, less individualistic) way of life. Mr. Nixon would not stay long enough to suffer culture shock or sinicization, but the Chinese view of reality may have gotten to him, even if briefly. It is a very rational view, given its premises, very experienced in the workings of human nature, addicted to self-discipline, and ready to subordinate the short term to the long—just the attitude needed for manipulating tribal chieftains who have to show quick results to their people back home.

Current realities of course had their impact, and Mr. Nixon's journey for peace from Washington to Peking no doubt succeeded roughly in proportion as the rest of our troops in Vietnam had already made their own journey for peace from Saigon to San Francisco.

Nevertheless, revolutionary China lives in the shadow of history just as much as we do. If our press and courts have recently been quoting a bill of rights that dates from the late Ch'ien-lung period, we could expect Chou En-lai to have been equally concerned about principles inherited from China's long experience in dealing with foreign visitors. The foreign visitor is a guest of the state, and like any guest should follow the rules of proper decorum: not for him to wag his finger argumentatively under the chairman's nose. There would be nothing like Vice President Nixon's kitchen-exhibit debate with Chairman Khrushchev. Dignity precedes advocacy.

Just as personal conduct reflects character, so state ceremonies symbolize the social order. Whether the Nixon visit inaugurated state-to-state relations or was still covered by a stretched-out "people's diplomacy," it did stress his personal quest for peace. He would have to go committed and live up to his promise.

Such visits create a crucial burden of advance preparation and negotiation. In the days of the Chinese empire that did business with the Taft administration, Western dignitaries in Peking sometimes found with dismay that words translated into Chinese changed their meaning in unfortunate ways. Personal "liberty" (*tzu-yu*) turned into "license." What do "self-determination" and "sovereignty" mean in Chinese today? How are they related? Russian ambassadors of the seventeenth century went through long hassles over the kowtow because it directly affected the basic structure of the state (*t'i-chih*). China's state structure today is very different, but still new and a bit amorphous, still evolving. One of its major components, "Mao Tse-tung Thought," has room in it for "American capitalistic imperialism" but it is not the seat of honor due a guest.

It is safe to say that a trip to Peking is the longest usually taken by an American president, intellectually speaking. Its preparation can hardly be overdone.

17

Solving Our "One China" Problem

The following analysis of our Taiwan problem and what to do about it preceded our mutual recognition of early 1979 by three years, yet the main structure of relationships suggested by history proved valid in the end. The article was published in September 1976.

• • •

Our China policy has been based on the ostensible agreement of Washington, Peking, and Taipei that there is but one China and that Taiwan is part of China. Since any teenager can see that this is a nonfactual statement, it must represent a diplomatic ideal. A moment's thought reveals, however, that it represents two opposing ideals, for both Peking and Taipei claim to be the one China. Washington is caught in the middle of a double-ended make-believe. To get out from between these rival, though extremely unequal, Chinese parties, the first step is to look at how we got into the situation.

For over a hundred years the United States has played a role in Chinese political life. Our first treaty of 1844 secured all the privileges for which Britain had fought the Opium War of 1840–1842. During the following century American merchants and missionaries were agents of change who helped to foster the great Chinese Revolution of modern times. In 1943 our unequal treaty privileges were formally abolished, but by that time we had become allies deeply involved in China's affairs while fighting Japan. Our mutual security treaty with the government of the Republic of China on Taiwan after 1954 has put us in the position of backing one side

This chapter appeared in the *Atlantic*, September 1976.

in a not-yet-concluded Chinese civil war. Like it or not, the American people have been and still are closely involved in Chinese life, more so than we generally realize.

The Nixon-Kissinger breakthrough of 1972, when Washington achieved closer relations with Peking, was long overdue. Ever since the Sino-Soviet split of 1960, it had been obvious that only a leader of the Republican Right could end a bankrupt American estrangement from the Chinese Revolution. The major motive compelling this act was the hope of equalizing the American contact with China and Russia in our triangular relationship so that the Soviets would not be middlemen between Peking and Washington. The Nixon–Chou En-lai Shanghai communiqué of February 1972 had the unusual merit of stating where the two sides disagreed as well as where they agreed. The exact terms of the normalization it envisaged remained to be worked out.

Continental versus Maritime

In general, the Chinese Revolution of modern times has involved two major areas, which we may call Continental China and Maritime China. Continental China is today a nation of farmers crowded upon the arable land. It has inherited the great Chinese imperial tradition of government by a bureaucracy controlled from the capital. It is an agrarian-bureaucratic empire busily engaged in updating itself.

Maritime China is younger, and yet its history goes back to the beginning of the Christian era. For almost two thousand years Chinese merchantmen, or junks, have plied the coastal waters of East Asia. For the last thousand years they have left a considerable record of trade and contact with Southeast Asia. These highly seaworthy compartmented vessels (the Chinese were pioneers in nautical technology, as in so much else) sailed the routes from Amoy and Canton to the Straits of Malacca and the Indian Ocean long before European ships arrived there. The first Portuguese who reached China in about 1514 did so by entering these routes of the Chinese junk trade. The Spaniards, Dutchmen, Englishmen, and Frenchmen who subsequently voyaged into Southeast Asia and eventually established colonies likewise found China merchant communities in the major seaports.

Maritime China thus long antedated the arrival of the European colonial powers. This maritime tradition stemming from South China was of course very different from that of Continental China. In overseas trade, individual enterprise is an essential ingredient, venture capital is required, and commercial calculations must predominate.

The growth of Maritime China, in short, was an East Asian counterpart of the expansion of Europe, which has spread steadily around the globe since the time of Columbus and still dominates the Western view of modern history. Yet so strong were the Chinese capabilities for seafaring and maritime trade that the seven big expeditions sent out by the Ming court in the early 1400s sailed to India and across the Indian Ocean to Arabia and Africa almost a century before the first Europeans succeeded in rounding the Cape of Good Hope and inaugurating the European maritime phase of world history. If they had wanted to, the Chinese could have made all Southeast Asia their colony long before the Europeans did so. China's inaction was due to the fact that overseas colonies had no appeal for the bureaucrats who ruled Continental China: their government in North China was not interested in sea trade and was preoccupied with the Mongol menace from Inner Asia.

European colonialism got its early bite from the commercial, even piratical, greed of rival rulers. Such crassness appalled the court of Peking, which continually asserted the old Confucian view that disesteemed trade and left it for officials to dominate. Both the Ming and the Ch'ing rulers had at times forbidden foreign trade entirely and closed down the seacoast in a vain effort to starve out coastal pirates and dissident regimes. In the seventeenth century, for example, Taiwan became the home of such a regime under the Sino-Japanese adventurer Cheng Ch'eng-kung (known in Western annals as Koxinga). In the eighteenth century Canton was made the sole port for European trade.

When British gunfire secured the opening of the treaty ports after 1842, greater scope was given to Maritime China's development; for the compradors who handled the inward and outward trade of the foreign merchants soon became Chinese merchants in their own right and emerged as a modern business and banking class. This growth, induced by foreign contact and treaty-port privilege, was part of China's modern economic development.

The Cantonese became the great middlemen between East and West. The Chinese migration to California under the famous Six Companies came mainly from this region. Out of it emerged the first professional revolutionary, Sun Yat-sen. American and British missionaries had their first success here. Yung Wing, who graduated from Yale in 1854, was Cantonese and so were most of the young trainees he succeeded in bringing to Hartford, Connecticut, in the 1870s under the Chinese Educational Mission as a pioneer effort in bicultural education.

Today China's foreign trade is conducted once again at Canton. Maritime China has grown. It now includes the British colony of Hong Kong, the Republic of Singapore, the Republic of China on Taiwan, and millions of other ethnic Chinese in Kuala Lumpur, Penang, Bangkok, Manila, Cholon, and elsewhere, who have given their allegiance to various of the newly independent states of Southeast Asia. In all these regions Chinese merchants and industrialists have led the way in an economic growth similar to that of Japan and South Korea, those other East Asian countries with a grounding in the Confucian ethic.

Measured by its results, this has been an economic revolution more potent per capita than anything in Continental China. It represents a peripheral integration of the Chinese into the international trading community on the basis of individual or corporate enterprise familiar to Americans and Western Europeans. While the total population of Maritime China may be only 25 or 30 million, its volume of activity in international trade exceeded for a time that of the People's Republic, with a population of more than a billion.

The Ideal of Unity

The paradox of Taiwan has been that its economy is part of Maritime China, but its political ideology is still that of Continental China. I refer to the One China concept, which has been the main ideal of all contenders for power on the mainland for more than two thousand years. For at least one-third of these two millennia, China has actually seen more than one political authority or organized state in existence. Nevertheless, the ideal of unity—all Chinese united under a single regime headed by the Son of

Heaven—has long been enshrined as the ultimate political goal. The realization of this ideal during the remaining two-thirds of the time has reinforced its potency.

The twentieth century, like previous eras, has demonstrated the desirability of China's unity as the means of avoiding civil war and the ravages of warlordism. Unity was patched up in 1912 to ward off Japanese intervention. It was nominally achieved in 1928 with great pride and rejoicing. Chiang Kai-shek rose through his devotion to this cause, even though the unification of China under the Nanking government of the 1930s was always imperfect. Unifying China to make it a great power against the encroachments of imperialism remained Chiang's lifelong ideal. Consequently his regime on Taiwan for almost three decades reiterated as an article of political faith its determination to reconquer the mainland.

The Republic of China under the Generalissimo's son, Chiang Ching-kuo, was morally obliged by filial piety to continue this fiction. Taiwan has been participating in the economic miracle of East Asian growth, but without shaking off its heritage of continental political ideals. This has been a remarkable instance of out-of-date thinking in the midst of up-to-date practice.

More important, the One China ideal on Taiwan kept the island locked in a position of unresolved civil warfare against the People's Republic. Americans who wanted to disentangle themselves from civil war in China confronted in their Chinese allies an idée fixe of religious proportions that could not be extirpated.

If Chiang Kai-shek's pride and devotion to his ideals had permitted it, the Nationalist regime in the early 1950s could easily have become an independent republic by renouncing any claims to the mainland and entering the United Nations on its merits. No doubt it would be there today. This would have been a solution based on self-determination, one that commends itself to Western thinking. Yet the facts of life over three decades hardly made a dent in Chinese political thought. Our friends in Taiwan still demanded that we support them as irreducible enemies of the People's Republic. Even today, "Two Chinas" is a dirty phrase in Taipei and Peking.

Peking does not make it any easier for us by reiterating in routinized slogans its determination to reconquer Taiwan as an inalienable part of the mother country. This we can understand and must take seriously. Rulers at Peking have gone to great lengths to eliminate rivals for power. The Yung-lo emperor of the Ming even sent expeditions overseas to seek out a refugee claimant. K'ang-hsi of the Ch'ing in a vast civil war wiped out the Ming remnants and took over Taiwan after forty years of independence. Elimination of rivals has been a necessary act of legitimization for Peking.

For more than thirty years, ever since Patrick J. Hurley and George C. Marshall tried to mediate in Chungking and Yenan, we have confronted civil strife in China. Explicitly since 1972 we have taken the pro forma position that the relations between the rival parties in China's civil war are for them to work out and not our responsibility. Yet history has tied us into the situation. Our mutual security treaty of 1954 with the Republic of China expressed the same American interest in trade and contact that motivated our original nineteenth-century intervention in Chinese life. The maritime trading world that was then the locus of Western and Japanese imperialism now harbors the hydra-headed multinationals and the "neo-imperialism" that communists continue to deplore and sometimes emulate. In fact, the Marxist verities, like those of free enterprise, are yielding to new facts.

How then are we to deal with these two antagonists?

On reflection we can see that the One China doctrine is one of those hoary Chinese devices for manipulating the unsophisticated barbarian. Our relations are like a romantic triangle in a novel: each of the ladies says, "Cleave to me only" and demands that we deny the other. On this basis we spent a quarter-century denying the existence of the People's Republic, winding up in Vietnam. Then Peking expected us to flop over completely and deny the existence of a longtime client and ally. But our world is pluralistic, and we could not fully satisfy either Chinese party.

The Uses of Fiction

In the face of the One China myth it does little good to point out that Taiwan spent fifty years, from 1895 to 1945, as a Japanese colony and then came under Nationalist control only as the Chinese Communist Party was taking over the mainland. Japanese colonialism developed Taiwan's economy, though not its cultural life, and American aid further assisted it. Most of all, the enterprise of Chinese mainlanders and Taiwanese alike has produced the present high living standard and productivity in international trade. As part of Maritime China, Taiwan has become less assimilable to the new continental society, in fact almost indigestible, by reason of being more highly capitalized and export oriented.

As for Taiwan's juridical independence, there were simply no Chinese supporters for the idea except an underground Formosan independence movement that never emerged as a practical alternative to the Nationalist government. Chinese patriots simply did not want to alienate a portion of the Chinese realm. Independence would not only reverse the Peking-Washington rapprochement; it would be a flagrant provocation that Peking could hardly overlook. In short, we Americans, coming from across the Pacific with very different political ideals, had to accept the traditional Chinese view of the unified Chinese state even while helping to create a disunified situation.

This left us obliged to resort to a fiction. There is no way that we could accomplish the return of Taiwan to mainland control, since the Republic of China was a viable regime, well armed and growing economically, actively intent on avoiding Peking's subjugation. To attempt the strangulation of such a regime would probably be ineffective.

Meanwhile, since we do not have to take One China as our primary article of political faith, we had no moral obligation to destroy Taiwan's separateness, but on the other hand we had a considerable moral responsibility because of our long association to see it continue. Half a century of recognition of the Nationalist government (since 1928) and a quarter-century of support of its island realm (since 1950) created a presumption of continuity and bonds of friendship that could not be shrugged off or lightly abandoned. The Taiwan community was, after all, part of our world, increasingly interconnected with us by trade, culture, education, and other lines. We share many ideals and institutional activities. It would be both infeasible and immoral to try to destroy the relationship.

Nevertheless, our relations with the vast People's Republic had been steadily developing in diplomatic contact, trade, travel, and the exchange of scientific and technical delegations. Peking admitted an increasing flow of American citizens, about two-thirds of Chinese descent, for tours of a few weeks. To backtrack in this growing contact with roughly a quarter of mankind, whose government is a nuclear power, was simply not a responsible or even moral proposition. No peaceful future for humanity could be assured without Peking-Washington collaboration. We shared a concern about the Soviet Union. At the very least we needed a degree of contact with China equal to our contact with the Soviets.

Normalization

Fortunately, Peking's interest in a Taiwan settlement is a bit different from Taipei's. When Soviet relations are seen as China's major foreign policy contradiction, differences with the United States are a minor contradiction—and this includes the American position in ("occupation of") Taiwan. Indeed, in realpolitik terms, the continued American presence in the western Pacific is an acceptable, even desirable, aspect of the Sino-American rapprochement, providing it supports stability (that is, opposes Soviet expansion there) and does not contravene China's long-term interests (for example, sovereignty over Taiwan). In this way the theoretical long-term interest of Peking differs from the practical short-term interest of Taipei. We can slip through the crack.

These considerations bring us to the question of the context of "normalization." Let us make a distinction in our policy thinking between theory and practice. Having accepted the theory of One China, we can hardly do less than acknowledge it in the form of the doctrine that Peking has sovereignty over Taiwan. However, being realists like the Chinese, we can properly accept the practical fact of the last eighty years, that Taiwan has had a separate regime, which we may call autonomous and which seems likely to remain so for the indefinite future no matter what we do. On this basis we can affirm that Peking's sovereignty over Taiwan is a deferred sovereignty, to be recognized in principle at all times but not as yet in practice.

As to our economic relations, if our recognition of Peking gives it most-favored-nation status in trade with the United States, then under the One China doctrine we can properly conclude that the same most-favored-nation treatment applies to Taiwan. Such would be the case with other aspects of our relations with Peking whenever the assertion of equal treatment for Taiwan might be convenient for us under the doctrine of One China. There are, of course, many legal arrangements that have to be worked out to give our Taiwan trade and contact a continuation of the status they have had. However, this is *our* problem. It concerns regulations we have created. Legal ingenuity can achieve the format we need. [This was to be done in the Taiwan Relations Act passed by Congress in early 1980.]

The Japanese model of making its Peking trade mission into an embassy and its Taipei embassy into a trade delegation has paved the way for us. The Japanese experience offers examples of these legal-economic arrangements, which have been worked out since 1972 by hard bargaining among the three parties concerned. Legal fictions make it possible for necessary Japanese consular functions to continue to be performed and for Japanese trade, travel, and investment to proceed in Taiwan.

The major thing lacking in the Japanese model is, of course, a security treaty, and our military arrangements concerning Taiwan are the crux of the matter. Both the security of Taiwan and the credibility of our security arrangements for Taiwan are of direct interest to Japan, where our defense commitment has helped that country's growth.

By the terms of the Nixon-Chou statement of 1972 and later promises, we are committed to reducing and withdrawing American forces from Taiwan; but this says nothing about the American bases in the Philippines and in Okinawa. Subic Bay is not an inconvenient distance from Taiwan, and a unilateral American declaration that we would defend the island against attack could remain as credible as ever. Our commitment would no longer be to defend a government from which we had withdrawn recognition, but to defend an area; and to avoid offense to Peking's idea of sovereignty, our unilateral public declaration pro forma might be simply to "maintain the stability of the western Pacific." The true meaning of this phrase would be spelled out less officially. We should assume that the Seventh Fleet is still capable of patrolling the Taiwan straits if it should seem necessary.

The hardest bargaining with Peking, perhaps informally, may come over the question of military supply to Taiwan's armed forces, but for a country supplying arms to half the world, some kind of supply through third parties or by other arrangements is not impossible.

The prospect in this settlement would be for a considerable growth of legal fictions. We may claim that within the One China that we acknowledge we are entitled to send consular officers to areas that cannot be reached from our embassy in Peking. Alternatively, we may have the American consulate general in Hong Kong extend its jurisdiction to nearby islands. In the early days of our China trade merchants acted as consuls in return for fees. International law has seen a tremendous variety of special arrangements in peculiar circumstances.

This kind of normalization would be designed to extricate us from an alliance with one side in an unsettled civil war. It would not settle the armed rivalry between Peking and Taipei, and our veiled but genuine commitment to defend Taiwan would leave us still intervening in Chinese politics. But it would be a forward step toward realism to recognize more explicitly that Continental China exists and that we are no longer enslaved by the ancient One China myth of the Chinese empire. It would free us to deal with the Chinese People's Republic on our common agenda looking toward global survival. Stabilizing the Taiwan question is only preliminary to much larger purposes.

All the necessary ad hoc and creative arrangements for the continuity of our relations with Continental and with Maritime China in the western Pacific should be entered into with a sense of practicality and no embarrassment. The necessary legal fictions should be regarded as subordinate matters of convenience, below the level of high policy and principle. Our future relations with Peking should justify themselves by the concrete advantages Peking receives. The American connection should prove its worth quite aside from what we may do concerning Taiwan. Despite the proliferation of legal fictions, none of them should menace the People's Republic of today or the long-term interests of the Chinese people. We can at all times explain their existence as a necessary response to the great ideal of One China, which happens not to be a workable fact.

One point is basic: to turn back from normalization would be a retrograde step toward the imperialism of the last century with all its dire potentialities of warfare. In practical terms we cannot accept either side of the One China claims of our Chinese friends in Peking and Taipei, although we acknowledge the existence of their One China ideal. Unless we are to be whipsawed eternally by their civil war, we must slip through the middle with a Taiwan arrangement of Peking's sovereignty (deferred) and Taipei's autonomy (limited) that will maintain stability in the western Pacific.

PART FOUR

The Cultural Revolution

Normalization of Washington-Peking relations in 1979 coincided with a great outpouring of Chinese accounts of the evils, indeed horrors, of the Cultural Revolution decade from 1966 to 1976.

The pendulum has swung anti-Maoist as we have heard the stories of persecution, torture, and destruction of modern Chinese intellectuals and officials during those years. The newly available record has facilitated foreign studies that give us a much more detailed and realistic understanding of what was going on in the People's Republic. This scholarly work is reflected here in reviews of Roderick MacFarquhar's study of the origins of the Cultural Revolution, while first-person accounts of experience are presented by William Hinton, Ken Ling, and Liang Heng.

18

Origins of the Cultural Revolution

The heart of China's twentieth-century revolution has been the revival of the Chinese state. Until the 1890s the Chinese empire had remained the most durable of the universal kingships of the ancient world. Its transformation into the state now known as the People's Republic has left the Chinese public saddled with a political order still deficient in our sort of civil liberties. To be sure, the old China had worked out certain customary limits to despotism, but how such limitations are to be institutionalized in the revived state remains uncertain. Now that China's great revolution is in remission and off the front page, scholars and journalists are reaching mature verdicts both about Mao's despotic part in it and about the quality of life that the new order has brought the Chinese people. Like tornado survivors, many Chinese have been wondering what hit them, and a flow of memoirs and more relaxed contact with outsiders have combined to give us a clearer view, at least for the moment.

Back in the late 1950s Mao's Great Leap Forward was quite opaque to us, especially in cold-war America. The lead in academic discussion of Mao's revolution was taken in London in 1960 by the founding of the *China Quarterly*. The first editor, Roderick MacFarquhar, spent eight years making this much-needed journal preeminent before he moved into full-time research on the origins of the Cultural Revolution, first at Columbia University and then

This review of Roderick MacFarquhar, *The Origins of the Cultural Revolution*, vol. 2: *The Great Leap Forward, 1958–1960* (New York: Columbia University Press, 1983), appeared in the *New York Review of Books,* January 19, 1984. Reprinted with permission from the *New York Review of Books.* Copyright © 1984 Nyrev, Inc.

at Chatham House (the Royal Institute of International Affairs in London). Mao's attempt in 1966–1969 to tear down and rebuild the edifice he had led in creating so shook the Chinese earth and so amazed the world that it has taken its place alongside 1789 and 1917 as one of the greatest of all the revolutions in which state power dissolved and had to be reconstituted.

The first volume of Mr. MacFarquhar's trilogy, *Origins of the Cultural Revolution, Contradictions among the People, 1956–1957*, came out in 1974. After it appeared, he served five years as a Labour member of Parliament. "Low-temperature British socialism of the 1970s," he says, "was a far cry from the utopian communism of China"; yet being an MP undoubtedly sharpened his understanding of the interplay between leaders and followers, ideology and policy, and, in his words, "politicians and bureaucrats, . . . conscience and compromise." Like the masterpieces of diplomatic history on the origins of the war in 1914 (before the enormous increase of communication made such work impossible), his second volume is based on a prodigious knowledge of where and when who said what. By sifting through the vast number of publications that accompanied Mao's last decade, 1966–1976, and the rehabilitations that followed, MacFarquhar has traced the genesis and vicissitudes of the Maoist policies that led to disaster. No one else has so succinctly and yet comprehensively summed up the Great Leap.

Chairman Mao's weak spot was that he couldn't stop doing what he was best at—mobilizing mass campaigns to attack the status quo. The result was a tragedy in three acts: first, the Anti-Rightist Campaign of 1957 that put so many of China's liberals and experts out of action; second, the Great Leap Forward of 1958–1960 that wrecked the economy; and third, the Cultural Revolution after 1965 that attacked intellectuals and the Chinese Communist Party. Granted that good things were accomplished along the way, Mao's overall influence after 1956 undoubtedly set China back. The fact that today's CCP subscribes to this verdict, while disconcerting, does not necessarily invalidate it. Mao's victims now in power acquired an all-too-solid basis for judgment.

Mr. MacFarquhar offers a single-minded though wide-ranging

dissection of the policymaking process. The CCP leaders were frenetically busy people, constantly moving about, yet continually conferring with one another. Having realized that China's agriculture could not provide the surplus for a Soviet-style heavy industrialization, they toured the country in early 1958 formulating plans to use China's biggest asset, her raw muscle power, for a Chinese-style breakthrough to modernize the economy. In January Mao conferred with local officials first in Hangchow near Shanghai, then in Kwangsi in the far south and in Canton, and then in Peking; in February in the northeast; in March in the southwest in Szechwan; in April in central China in Wuhan, then in Changsha, and in Canton again; and in May back in Peking, where Mao and Liu Shao-ch'i, his deputy, formally launched the Great Leap Forward.

At all these conferences Mao and his Politburo colleagues made pronouncements that allow the indefatigable MacFarquhar to trace the growth of their policies. Repeatedly he finds Mao in the lead, pushing for adventurous and grandiose innovations. For example, the origin of the communes lay in the fact that the new Agricultural Producers' Cooperatives (APCs), which in 1957 averaged only 164 families apiece, were too small to mobilize the massed rural muscle power needed to build dams, dikes, ditches, and other water conservancy works. To meet this need, APCs began to combine to form bigger units. The process was encouraged but not given a name at the early 1958 conferences.

In April twenty-seven APCs in Honan merged their 9,369 families into one regimented work unit. In June Mao began suddenly to call for communes to be the basic units of the nation, combining "agriculture, industry, commerce, culture and education, and militia, i.e., the whole people armed." By the end of August the Politburo conference at the seaside resort of Peitaiho, on the basis of very limited and brief experience, made communes the official all-purpose ten-thousand-person building blocks for a new rural China. They quite disregarded, as MacFarquhar points out, "the ideological and intra-bloc implications" of this utopian leap into a degree of communal living not previously achieved in the communist world. Moscow would have to denounce it.

The utopian fever with which Mao and his colleagues became infected in the summer of 1958 had its international aspect: Khrushchev visited Mao on July 31. They failed to agree on naval co-operation on the China coast, but on August 23 Mao on his own began the bombardment of the Nationalists on the offshore island of Quemoy. When this precipitated a confrontation with the United States, Gromyko flew to Peking. Soviet support of China was publicly promised only after Mao had given up the enterprise of recovering Quemoy. "The seeds of further bitterness between Moscow and Peking had been sown"; Mao and company felt confirmed in the idea of going it alone.

Utopianism soon took over. The retreat over Quemoy was masked by an enormous "everyone-a-soldier" movement to organize militia. There were 220 million soldiers enrolled by January 1959, but not many with weapons and fewer still with ammunition. Meanwhile everyone was to eat in mess halls under a "free-supply" system. Everyone was to labor voluntarily with no need of materialistic "bourgeois" wages. Education was to be combined with manual labor and factories with schools, to produce what Liu Shao-ch'i called "proletarian intellectuals" both red and expert. The national fever rose to a dramatic delirium in the backyard steel-smelting campaign. MacFarquhar presents poignant testimony on the production frenzy that in late 1958 engulfed hundreds of millions of people—essential cooking pots were melted down to feed the furnaces, commune farming was militarized like warfare, grain production figures were doubled and redoubled (which led to collecting grain quotas so large that peasants had not enough left to live on), deep plowing destroyed the soil. There were many other inanities such as campaigns to kill all the sparrows, while bumper crops rotted in the fields because people were too busy to harvest them.

By mid-1959 it was obvious that production figures had been wildly inflated, the steel campaign was a bust, agriculture was disrupted, and farmers were exhausted and undernourished. The climax of MacFarquhar's drama, "High Noon at Lushan," is the July 1959 conference at which the doughty head of the army, General P'eng Te-huai, never a Mao sycophant, laid the blame at the door of the great leader. Mao's defensive counterblast blew General P'eng into retirement. The Politburo members were all parties to the crisis: between Mao and P'eng, they had to choose Mao. The result was to prolong the Great Leap with a sort of "revivalism" and so compound the disaster, a foretaste of the Cultural Revolution after 1965.

How could all this happen? Such harebrained romanticism would not mobilize American farmers in Fargo or Fresno or even Provo. The Great Leap was so bizarre a triumph of revolutionary fervor over common sense that one wishes the historical literature were adequate to connect it with its antecedents in Chinese history. Unfortunately the institutional history of China remains still underdeveloped. The great tradition of statecraft (*ching shih*), how the bureaucrats customarily organized and manipulated the populace, is neglected while researchers today swarm into social history as more suited to current concerns.

Institutional and historical perspective on the Great Leap would no doubt begin with the parts of the written dynastic histories dealing with the economy. These detail how new regimes, upon reunifying China, commonly mobilized corvée labor for great public works (and often wore it out), how they assigned peasants, for example, "equal field" allotments of land, and organized them into responsibility groups for mutual surveillance. Dozens of ingenious devices, like "ever-normal granaries" in each locality or soldier-farmer encampments on the frontiers, stand in the record unstudied. The question of how these clever schemes of scholar-administrators actually worked out in practice remains largely unanswered. They represented the ruler's unquestioned prerogative to structure the life of the people by personal example, sumptuary regulations, moral exhortation, and condign punishments.

We know that Mao praised the first emperor of 221 B.C. who buried scholars and burned their bamboo books. We know that the first emperor of the Ming after 1368 planted millions of trees and had his ministers ceremoniously beaten in court. In fact he became paranoid, killed his chief minister, and terrorized the scholars. When the record is mastered, I suspect it will be evident that what Mao attempted was in the spirit of many predecessors, and that he often used their methods—except that Mao had some new devices and was in more of a hurry.

MacFarquhar concludes with a chilling demonstration that the Great Leap indeed built up heavy industry but at tremendous human cost, especially among the peasantry: in 1960, a bad crop year, the mortality rate doubled. "Anywhere from 16.4 to 29.5

million extra people died during the leap, because of the leap." The proximate cause of the disaster was "the Mao factor . . . Without Mao there would have been no leap . . . no communes . . . no mass steel campaign . . . no revival of the leap." True enough, and spoken like a political scientist exhaustively versed in the record. But perhaps a historian can add: without the ancient Chinese monarchy, there would have been no Mao.

19

Revolution and Reform
in a Shansi Village

When Bill Hinton went out to China for the second time in 1945 to work under the United States Office of War Information, he was a big, outgoing, practical young man, quite unafraid of any "ism," right or left. After Harvard and Cornell, he brought to revolutionary China the same humane enthusiasm for collective endeavor and technical skills with which his mother, Carmelita Hinton, had founded her progressive school at Putney, Vermont. In 1947 he went to China for the third time under the United Nations Relief and Rehabilitation Administration as a tractor technician. In the spring and summer of 1948 he accompanied a Chinese Communist Party work team that investigated land reform in the village of Long Bow on the arid, rocky tableland of Shansi province west of Peking.

With two interpreters Hinton collected extensive notes on how the villagers under communist guidance had carried through a social and economic revolution, destroying the power of the old gentry-landlord elite, working out everyone's class status, and dividing up the community's property to make a new, more equitable society. When Hinton finally came back to the United States in 1953, the United States Customs Bureau and later a congressional committee protected us by seizing his notes. It took him five years and a lot of legal expense to get them back. The book that he finally produced in 1966, *Fanshen: A Documentary of Revolution in a Chinese Village,* was an inside account, the farthest inside that any foreigner had been in China's peasant revolution, full of conversation and deft descriptions of people.

This chapter appeared in the *Boston Sunday Globe,* May 15, 1983, as a review of William Hinton, *Shenfan: The Continuing Revolution in a Chinese Village* (New York: Random House, 1983).

By the time Chinese-American relations thawed in 1971, Bill Hinton was a farmer in Pennsylvania. He went back to China at Premier Chou En-lai's invitation for a seven-month tour, finally including Long Bow village in the late summer and fall. As before, he was an observer attached to a Communist Party work team, but this time he was helped by his able and vivacious daughter, Carma, who had been born in Peking and grown up there during the revolution. With her interpreting, Bill Hinton filled ten thick notebooks with interviews and impressions, "many of them contradictory."

Shenfan is the result, a massive work about scores of individuals, their petty schemes, loves and hates, hopes and troubles, like a Victorian novel. "Fanshen" meant "turning over" to the new order; "Shenfan" means "deep plowing," the vicissitudes under the new order. Where the earlier work was upbeat, a victorious struggle into a new day, this second volume is more somber, about struggles with persistent problems. It traces the history of Long Bow's villagers from 1948 to 1971. These twenty-three years cover four successive phases of revolution that affected the Long Bow peasants in different ways.

The first phase after 1948 was the process of collectivization. Land reform had distributed land more equally among the peasant cultivators but left the party facing a nationwide problem—whether to permit the rise of a rich peasant economy through the more enterprising achievements of some, or to move everyone toward a more egalitarian collectivism. Mao pressed for collectivization. The move toward it went in stages by way of mutual aid teams; cooperatives in which farmers shared according to their input of land, animals, tools, and labor; and finally, production teams that bought up all property and paid the farmers by the work points they earned. After 1956, with the land markers all removed, no one could find his old plots and everyone was in it together.

In Long Bow the villagewide brigade had seven teams, six for agriculture and one for sideline occupations, and grain production had almost doubled. Meanwhile the state took over the grain trade and prohibited migration to the cities. This made it easier to collect the farm surplus and put everyone on grain rations.

China's drive for collective farming in the 1950s is of special interest a generation later. Deng Xiaoping's new "responsibility system" of individual contracts and family farms aims to revive the work incentive and raise production. But now we hear of villagers dismantling their collective installations to the point of cutting down trees and stealing the doors and windows of schoolhouses.

The second phase in Long Bow was the Great Leap Forward of 1958, a mass campaign to industrialize the countryside by mobilizing muscle power. Hinton finds there was an exhilaration about the Great Leap which, although it did not last, was nevertheless extraordinary and genuine at the time. The whole idea of making big public installations by mobilization of labor was not only an old tradition but also part of China's modernization effort. It involved learning about electricity and applied mechanics.

The Great Leap was undone by excesses when the "Communist wind" blew so hard that complete egalitarianism was sought without regard for vested rights or mutual benefit. Wild claims were trumpeted as tremendous victories, and the bureaucrats exaggerated their statistics till they became nonsense. Worse than that, the cadres in charge became intoxicated and separated from reality, proposing schemes and demanding compliance when only frustration could be achieved. Conflicting orders and overenthusiasm exhausted the peasantry and eventually they became demoralized. "In the long run the biggest casualty of all was the habit of telling the truth." Afterward came poor crops and semistarvation.

Long Bow's next revolutionary experience was in the Four Clean movement of the early 1960s and the Socialist Education Campaign that followed. In both the effort to induce "class struggle" as a further stage of allegedly necessary revolution failed to enlist popular support. The continued imposition of class status and its inheritance by children of "rightists" seemed to be generally accepted, but the criteria remained too vague to be precisely applied. These rectification movements opened the door for personal animosities based on local rivalries and other noneconomic considerations.

The final phase was Chairman Mao's so-called Cultural Revolution beginning in 1966. Since "class struggle" against the newly entrenched bureaucrats did not catch fire from above, Mao fielded his teenage Red Guards to "make revolution" from below. *Shenfan* provides a narrative of the Cultural Revolution factionalism in Shansi province as a whole and in the southeastern plateau, as well as in Long Bow village itself.

Mao's call to "bombard the headquarters" and the seizures of power by revolutionary rebels were met by a similar fielding of Red Guards and deployment of factional forces in defense of the bureaucracy. As leading figures in power were pulled down and new figures took over, the means of struggle steadily escalated from demonstrations and mass meetings to fisticuffs and beatings and eventually to the use of firearms.

Civil war in full form occupied many regions, and then the army was drawn into politics and lost some of its neutral posture. A leadership emerged in Long Bow that was cynical and opportunist and rapidly became corrupt and tyrannical. By 1971, when Hinton joined the work team trying to rectify this situation, the revolution seemed played out.

As Bill Hinton sat in on work team meetings in 1971, he reflected on the continuities and discontinuities of the revolution. The new party and government structures again separated the bureaucratic cadre class from the ordinary citizens. People now spoke their minds at a great rate, but their claims to have rights were always subject to the overriding and alleged supremacy of the group interest, and in the end of the Chinese state represented by the party.

Hinton also found an inveterate tendency toward ritual denunciation and righteous indignation that admitted no compromise. These qualities provided the stuff of factionalism, into which the Cultural Revolution fell to its disaster. He was surprised and perplexed at the way small groups, once a movement got started, soon joined up to form two opposing organizations.

As in England's War of the Roses, the groups were based on personal ties and loyalty to factional leaders. Each faction would call the other counterrevolutionary, a fighting word and a justification for execution of those found guilty. The pressure for conformity was so strong that staying out of such lineups became very difficult, and yet joining up in righteous struggle against an opposing group had little ideological significance. Historically, of course, this factionalism goes back to the tradition of village feuds in Chinese peasant life.

Meanwhile bureaucratism continued to make its demands. For example, wide furrows were commanded, and interplanting of wheat and corn. As an experienced farmer, Bill Hinton was not impressed. Interplanting meant that neither tractors nor carts could be taken down the rows of crops, and consequently farmers had to carry compost on shoulder poles, thereby packing the soil again so that a field might have to be hoed several times, all extremely uneconomic of labor power.

Another strategem demanded by the cadres from on high was the raising of piglets by every family, a policy that ate into the grain supply. At another time sideline activities such as pig raising were denounced as "the tail of capitalism in the countryside" and orders were given to kill all the pigs. Vain, ignorant cadres, though lacking in farm experience, nevertheless gave orders—about plowing, planting, seeds, and tools—that produced countless disasters. Bureaucratism menaced collectivism.

Yet Bill Hinton is left wondering today whether the revival of family farming and the dismantling of the collective structures built up with such travail can serve China adequately for the future.

"In the past I took it for granted that the old Chinese state grew up to serve and protect the interests of the landlord class. It now seems clear that this traditional state apparatus developed in time into an autonomous entity . . . The Chinese revolution of the twentieth century thoroughly uprooted . . . the landlords . . . It nevertheless re-created a bureaucratic infrastructure uncannily reminiscent of those built by past dynasties."

In short, an absolutely tremendous development has occurred in China, but less change than you might expect.

20

How to Be a Red Guard

The Red Guards with their red armbands marched through the great T'ien-an Men Square in Peking by the hundreds of thousands, waving aloft their little red books of quotations from Chairman Mao. They were boys and girls, mainly from urban middle schools. Their mobilization in the late summer and fall of 1966 startled the world. By the middle of 1968, when they had to be disbanded, they had proved to be a formidable engine of destruction. These student youths, caught up in a fervent adoration of the portly chairman, were urged by him to learn revolution by making revolution. In his name they were out to cleanse Chinese society of all things old, both artifacts and ideas. I doubt if anything like it had been seen since the Children's Crusade.

In their two years of existence the Red Guards went through a traumatic cycle. They did their Long Marches by traveling free on the railways to all parts of the country. They enjoyed a nationwide spirit of fellowship as well as the prestige of power. However, though beginning as cleansers and saviors of the nation and its revolution, they soon found themselves organized in groups from their schools, which quickly became factions in competition with other factions. They were nominally managing all kinds of public enterprises, having supplanted party administrators and municipal and factory officials. Having taken on the management of local politics, they developed political interests. Again, their factional

This chapter is based mainly on a review of Ken Ling, Ivan London, and Miriam London, *The Revenge of Heaven: Journal of a Young Chinese* (London: Putnam, 1971), that was published in the *New York Review of Books*, February 24, 1972. Reprinted with permission from the *New York Review of Books*. Copyright © 1972 Nyrev, Inc.

conflict among themselves progressed from demonstrations to fist-icuffs and then the use of weapons. By the summer of 1968, whole cities were riven by Red Guard battles. At first the provincial mil-itary forces stood on the sidelines holding the ring, though some-times supplying arms. In the end they had to be called in to sup-press the Red Guard battles and restore order. For the youths involved, the trauma was completed when Mao sadly berated them for having let him down and began the program of sending them to the countryside. Although they "volunteered" under group pressure, the effect of leaving the city to live and work at the peas-ant level was a frightful challenge and for many quite devastating. While Mao Tse-tung had inspired and at first directed the move-ment, it had got out of hand and died with a whimper.

Some Red Guards who were in a geographically fortunate po-sition avoided being "sent down" by escaping to Hong Kong and Taiwan. *The Revenge of Heaven* is a participant's account that may fascinate the reader, like evidence at a murder trial. The young narrator is somewhere between an old life and a new one, evidently buffeted by consideration of personal security, pride, patriotism, disillusionment, and hope for commercial gain.

The pseudonymous Ken Ling deposes that he became a Red Guard in July 1966, played a leading role in Red Guard struggles for power in Amoy and Foochow, traveled to Shanghai, Tsingtao, Peking, the northeast, Taiyuan, Lanchow, and elsewhere in late 1966, then for the rest of 1967 helped to lead one Amoy faction against another. After the Red Guards' resort to firearms in late 1967 began to produce serious casualties among factions, the lead-ers were finally hailed to Peking and deprived of power in February 1968. Ling defected by swimming to a Quemoy outpost in July. On Taiwan he produced an account comprising half a million Chi-nese characters and spent more than three hundred hours in inter-views with Ivan London's research team, which now gives us this book as an I-was-there story of the Cultural Revolution by a local leader in it.

A couple of funny things happened to Ling's reminiscences on their way to publication. First, Mao and his ideological exhorta-tions are denigrated throughout: the little red book is only a gim-mick; seeing Mao is unimpressive; and the only question for the Red Guard leaders is whether they can use Mao more than he uses them. This of course flies in the face of a vast amount of evidence from European and other observers about the ecstasy and fanaticism of the millions of Mao-inspired youth in the early phases of the Red Guard movement. Such extirpation of the idealistic central dynamic of the Cultural Revolution is, of course, what one would expect in a document from Taiwan, where the civil war is still (or was until recently) a sacred trust.

A second thing that happened to Ling's reminiscences was the injection of an improbable and highly saccharine love story. One is reminded of the American translator adding a spurious boy-gets-girl ending to Lao She's tragedy, *Rickshaw Boy* (New York: Reynal and Hitchcock, 1945), which no doubt helped it to become a bestseller in middle America. The Red Guard heroine is called Mei-mei, perhaps the commonest girl's appellation in China, for it means "little sister." She is a genuine China doll—dainty, accomplished, upper class, fastidious, and so wedded to the old morality that although she and Ling are madly in love and spend much time breaking up the "Four Olds" on all sides, in an atmosphere of general violence, rape, and mayhem, they never make it together. A real ideal dream girl, not of this world.

However, Ling's account of the Red Guards' rise to power in Fukien, on his home ground, where fanciful invention is not required by his script, has a fascinating verisimilitude. When his group of 304 Amoy Eighth Middle School youngsters are refused truck transport to Foochow by the Party Committee, they start marching under strict self-orders not to eat or drink anything. By the time they have walked 31 kilometers in the hot sun and ten marchers have fainted, the party authorities feel obliged to send them on by truck. Later in the "8-29" (August 29) fight at Foochow, when this Amoy group, though outnumbered, challenges the party authorities, "the Foochow Red Guards adopted the tactic of 'isolate and attack.'" Ling is surrounded by six or seven girls who bite, scratch, or pinch him in thirty-seven places including amidships. The reader feels that Ling speaks from experience.

The Red Guard violence begins within the schools, where teachers are humiliated in dunce's caps and incarcerated in a "black den" as "cow ghosts and snake demons," using the metaphoric slogans of the day. A great deal of callous torture and obscenity is recounted. We have little reason to doubt that China's turmoil saw this kind of personal savagery, but when the Maoist rationale is strained out, it becomes mere violence for its own sake or, as the Soviets say, "hooliganism," instead of violence in the name of virtue, which others report as typical of the Cultural Revolution.

In the next phase the Red Guards break out into the public scene to smash the Four Olds. The Amoy Eighth Middle School team is subdivided into twenty-two small groups with names like "Kill-the-Tiger team" or "Freeze-the-Flies-to-Death team." They begin to rampage through the city under the sanction of Mao's slogan "Rebellion is justified," committing the excesses that were so well publicized and shocking at the time. Soon they escalate their aims to a third stage, aiming at power. They organize a fortress headquarters and its specialized functions; acquire jeeps, trucks, and loudspeakers; and eventually overthrow the Party Committee and take on some of the functions of local government. All this time the army stays on the sidelines and even the police do not defend themselves with gunfire. Finally the movement degenerates into pure factionalism, one organization against another, and they resort more and more to violence until the military crack down and disband them. This first-person account is both chilling and poignant.

21

Mao's Struggle for a New Educational System

Mao's last decade was as full of confusion and surprises as the 1790s in France. In size and complexity the Cultural Revolution was of course a much bigger event than the French Revolution. At any rate, it will be studied from many angles for a long time to come. Probably its most arresting feature in retrospect was its disastrous attack on learning and intellectuals in the very land that had exalted scholarship and invented civil service examinations thirteen hundred years before. In fact, the two were not unconnected—learning was attacked in China because it seemed to be so entrenched in the establishment. This historical circumstance makes the Cultural Revolution hard to understand without reference to history.

Because the twentieth-century Chinese educational system is roughly comparable with those in other developing countries, Jonathan Unger's *Education under Mao* began as part of a project sponsored by Great Britain's Institute of Developmental Studies to seek "solutions to the 'diploma disease' that has beset the educational systems of many of the Third World countries." To study the violent Cultural Revolution as a manifestation of diploma disease is like treating toxic shock under a diagnosis of chickenpox.

This chapter is based on a review of Jonathan Unger, *Education under Mao: Class and Competition in Canton Schools, 1960–1980* (New York: Columbia University Press, 1982); Susan L. Shirk, *Competitive Comrades: Career Incentives and Student Strategies in China* (Berkeley: University of California Press, 1982); and Robert Taylor, *China's Intellectual Dilemma: Politics and University Enrolment, 1949–1978* (Vancouver: University of British Columbia Press, 1981). The review appeared as "'Red' or 'Expert'?" in the *New York Review of Books*, December 2, 1982. Reprinted with permission from the *New York Review of Books*. Copyright © 1982 Nyrev, Inc.

But never mind. We used to give money to China research in the name of national defense.

To study China as part of the Third World presumably answers the need for all social scientists to be comparative, whether or not comparison explains anything. Susan Shirk's *Competitive Comrades* begins by noting that Mao's political moralism resembled that of Rousseau and other revolutionary movements (Puritanism, fascism, satyagraha, Islam, Marxism) that have advocated "total ethical transformations." A structuralist, Shirk says that "policy-generated structure is a better starting point for understanding behavior" than is the usual concern for psychological tendencies passed down through cultural tradition. One is tempted to ask her about the "culture-generated policy" that must lie behind the "policy-generated structure."

To make an exception of an area like China on the grounds of cultural differences fostered by a long history is not feasible in her kind of social science. To be sure, Susan Shirk notes that Mao's "moralism also was rooted in ancient Chinese tradition," and Unger seems historically well informed. His Appendix B notes that the Chinese literati "have always been associated with the political realm." Both writers make a polite bow to history but prefer to go into contemporary situations and outward in space rather than backward in time.

In their comparative and contemporary world view, China stands, by definition and by its own policy statements, in the ranks of the Third World countries. If we look at the facts, China does indeed stand there, in size and age an elephant among rabbits. Comparing China with Ghana no doubt has theoretical value. To argue that China is a "nation imprisoned by its history," as has been said, may of course be only another way of showing that sinologists are imprisoned by their China. But if we grant that harping on China's exceptionalism is parochially antiscientific, does this require that social scientists studying China try to fly blind historically? Does the behavioral approach rule out the genetic? Neither diploma disease nor Third World comparisons can account for the ferocity of the Maoist "class struggle" against the educational system.

To understand the origins of the Cultural Revolution we have to get some picture of the establishment it was attacking—not merely the party apparatus under Liu Shao-ch'i and Deng Xiaoping, but the Chinese bureaucratic habits Mao saw reappearing in the party. This leads naturally back to the Chinese invention of bureaucratic government two thousand years ago in the Han period, and the subsequent Chinese inventions of paper, printed books, and civil service examinations. By one thousand years ago, under the Sung dynasty, the examination system was a major arm of the state. Down to its abolition in 1905 it recruited the indoctrinated elite needed to govern the masses—how to govern peasants having become the great Chinese specialty in the world's most stable empire.

Where the Han had governed, say, 45 million peasants, the Ch'ing dynasty by 1900 was governing 300 million. Mao's successors today have 800 million or more—more farmers than you can find in the Americas, Europe, Japan, and the USSR combined.

This is what made education so important. Once in power in 1949 Mao needed to establish institutions for his regime through an indoctrinated elite such as the examination system had provided until 1905 (when he was twelve years old). He needed persons trained in his state orthodoxy who could propagate his new social order. Since party dictatorship had supplanted dynastic despotism as China's system of government in the 1920s, Mao's new elite had to be the Chinese Communist Party and its cadres, "reds" committed to his revolution. How to train such activists through China's educational system was a top priority.

It was not as easy as one might think. Until 1905 those who wanted to rise in the world had prepared for the old government examinations through private instruction in family and villages, and the elite had also used some thousands of semiofficial academies, which were the only residential schools or colleges in the country. The examination system's many-tiered, multichanneled structure had fostered an "examination psychology" among men of worldly ambition, but it was not a public-school system and did not aim at mass education. It rewarded literary skill, orthodox thinking, and conservative morality if not bigotry, while offering little chance for technical specialization. But during the 1911–1949 interregnum of central power between the end of the Ch'ing dynasty and the takeover by the CCP, Chinese education had been rebuilt in modern style, first by organizing a school system on Japanese lines and then by setting up universities on largely liberal American models.

The products of this modern education, China's twentieth-century intellectuals trained in science, technology, and the humanities, have been generally regarded as the nominal and sometimes spiritual successors of the traditional literati who won degrees in the old examination system. But this appearance is deceptive. China's literati after 1905 had in fact proliferated and branched out to form a new intelligentsia that included journalists, writers, teachers, doctors, engineers, and all the other professionals. They were no longer mainly a talent pool of local gentry when out of office or civil servants when selected for state employment. They did not think with one mind; nor were they primarily devoted to propagating the state ideology and its doctrines of virtuous conduct. They were specialists, modern people whom leaders like Liu Shao-ch'i and Deng Xiaoping after 1949 wanted to recruit as experts to help modernize China.

In short, it can be argued that the old examination degree–holders' functional successors were not such modern experts but were really the new red party cadres, a selected elite morally committed to the leader of the state and his vision of egalitarian revolution. For many centuries government in China had relied on indoctrinated cadres. They were not a Soviet invention, even though many of them thought they were. The fact that their ideas were now anti-Confucian could not change their function in the system. In some ways China's modern diversified intelligentsia were more novel than the CCP cadres. Thus the stage was set for the "class struggle" of red versus expert.

Viewed in this historical perspective, the Cultural Revolution was a product of more than an old man's frustration. It represented an inevitable conflict between the new ruler's customary need for ideological loyalty and the modernizer's need for special skills. Mao was highly traditional in conceiving of education as indoctrination. He deplored even the modern specialization that the CCP modeled on the Soviet system in the 1950s, because it gave the specialist a basis for being independent-minded and potentially unorthodox, at least in his own specialty. But since the revolution to bring the peasant masses into politics was so long overdue in China, Mao faced the problem that school examinations would continue to favor the children of educated parents, and specialists recruited to modernize China's technology would seldom come from the peasantry.

Mao had adopted the peasants' ancient distrust of the literati as hangers-on of bureaucrats and local magnates. He also inherited the five-foot shelf of Chinese attacks on the old examination system from Wang An-shih (1021–1086) in the Sung to Ku Yen-wu (1613–1682) in the Ch'ing. Education in China had had a long and sophisticated history that had left residual attitudes and assumptions—for example, that brain and brawn are naturally separate, that learning is to serve society through the state, and that orthodoxy is essential to order. This makes one wonder whether diploma disease in China is most meaningfully seen as a contemporary Third World ailment or as a millennial examination disease encysted in the Chinese body politic.

Once launched on their research, both Unger and Shirk did an exemplary job of interviewing in Hong Kong, where the lengthy and circumstantial accounts of cooperative informants can be cross-checked for verisimilitude. Jonathan Unger concentrated on Canton, looking at events there within the framework of national policies and campaigns. In addition to the Canton press and documents, he relied on 191 interview sessions in 1975–1976 with forty-three former residents of China. From these interviews he distilled tables of data on the composition of each respondent's school class, since class members stayed together for years on end and had to know all about each other. Susan Shirk began interviewing in Hong Kong in 1969. Especially in 1971, as well as in 1978–1979, she interviewed in her own Mandarin, and in depth, thirty-one students and three teachers, all refugees from Chinese urban high schools (*chung hsueh*). Her methodological appendix makes a persuasive case for her intensive rather than extensive procedure.

The efficacy of this skillful interviewing is highlighted by the contrast with Robert Taylor's study, *China's Intellectual Dilemma*, which he seems to have based entirely on library research and on his own faith in what Mao was up to. Taylor lists thirty-three Chinese newspapers and periodicals in addition to all the usual books, journals, and translation services. Combing this evidence, he constructs a narrative of the struggle between the wily Liu Shao-ch'i's persistent interest in "functional specificity" (which tends to revive individualism) and "Mao's formulation of the proletarian intellectual concept."

Robert Taylor is history minded and opens with a historical summary. But as he goes along describing the eligibility and preparation of candidates, the administration of university enrollment, the selection system, and the elite-mass structure, it becomes apparent that he cannot get his feet on factual ground. His selected evidence deals in ideological goals and aspirations, regulations and their rationale, fragmentary data and estimates, denunciations of evils—in short, in exhortation rather than fact. The understanding of the Cultural Revolution that he gets through the contemporary Chinese press is about like the understanding of the American economy one would obtain from remarks overheard at a bankers' convention. Evidently carried away by the Maoist euphoria of the late 1960s, Taylor recounts how Mao wanted to put "politics in command," "achieve the integration of education and society," and create "proletarian intellectuals." In 1958 Mao hoped

the educational system would cease to exist as a separate entity when it became one with the part-time system, itself integrated with society . . . By 1965 it had become clear to Mao Tse-tung and his supporters that the only way in which the Liuist subversion of the Party's educational philosophy could be prevented was by the closure of universities and institutes, with the concomitant destruction of the education system . . . By 1970 the link between education and society through production was being forged in three ways: (i) by worker participation in the university, (ii) by teacher participation in production, and (iii) by student participation in labour . . . The integration of education and society was to be achieved through the interchangeability of roles of teachers, students, and workers.

Such incantations, as we know, created a real shambles. Just as Mao knew little economics ("I understand nothing about industrial planning," he confessed in 1959), so this gobbledygook makes it plain that he did not understand science and technology either. The traditional imperative imposed upon a new ruler of China, to achieve an orthodox consensus supporting his revolutionary regime, led Mao to exalt the peasant over the scholar (proletariat over bourgeoisie), and this ensnared him in a struggle against modern learning.

This struggle did not begin at once. During the 1950s the preliberation system had continued in place. Students competed at four successive levels—to enter primary school (six years), junior high (three years), senior high (three), and university (four). The Chinese fixation on degree status as the measure of success was as strong as ever. The government examinations before 1905 had been at the county, prefectural, provincial, capital, and palace levels. Now the revolution had reasserted the primacy of ideology, which formerly had been ensured by mastery of the Confucian classics, but which the liberal curriculum of the twentieth century had abandoned.

To reestablish an orthodoxy that would buttress its revolutionary government, the CCP had long since set up categories of class status. Though announced in Marxist terms, this categorization was actually what the founder of the Ming, a great organizer, had done, like emperors before him: after 1368, farm families, artisan families, and military families, as well as official families, were all registered, and sons were expected to continue their father's status. The Ming founder, declaring that "the primary thing in government is transformation through education," also ordered that "schools be established in all prefectures, subprefectures and counties, each with a state-supported teaching staff and state-supported students." (Quoted from Charles O. Hucker's 1978 book, *The Ming Dynasty: Its Origins and Evolving Institutions.*)

During the 1950s socialist China could do no less. The CCP rated school applicants according to three criteria: family class origin, political behavior, and academic performance. Class origins ranged from good (CCP revolutionaries, soldiers, workers, peasants) to midlevel (former middle peasants and urban white-collar) to bad (capitalists, rich peasants, landlords, "rightists"). In each district the school best staffed and equipped was made a "keypoint" school, into which came especially children of CCP officials (of good class origin) and of midlevel intelligentsia (of high academic capacity from their parental environment). Working-class youths filtered into the poorer high schools and into a separate echelon of vocational schools that fed their graduates directly into factories.

The stress on class origin and political activism aimed to check the intelligentsia's continuing to staff the new China with their liberal-minded children. Many expedients were tried to produce worker-peasant-soldier graduates: setting up part-time and people-managed schools, shortening the educational ladder, simplifying textbooks, and reducing requirements. Another reform effort was to reduce the rote memorizing that had been inculcated, Unger says, by the special nature of Chinese writing, the belief in literary models, and the tradition of promoting ethical behavior through classical moral maxims. Teachers assumed there was "a single truth that should be taught—the 'correct line'"—and they set frequent tests. To combat this tendency, key-point schools and universities experimented with open-book examinations. Unger mentions the program for rural half-farming/half-study schools, as well as the program to compress the twelve-year system into ten years as in the Soviet Union. By 1965 both had petered out, "pulled back toward the standards set by the higher-school exams and toward the curriculum of the regular academic track because that curriculum and its exam system defined what the public and school staffs took to be the *legitimate* system of schooling."

And why not? Would one not expect the examination route ("meritocracy," as Shirk calls it) to be the norm to the modern Chinese public? Unger does not go into the matter, but with a bit more concern for history he could have reminded us that meritocracy in China antedates Christianity in the West, and the Chinese examination system is far older than trial by jury in Britain. Its legitimacy as the main channel for getting ahead in the world is deeply embedded in the Chinese experience. Their counterparts of our folk figures from young Lochinvar to Li'l Abner were generally examination candidates. (Huck Finn of course can be rated as a failed scholar.) Before the time of Caesar or Christ, the emperors had begun to examine candidates recommended by high officials. Long before Charlemagne the Chinese system was firmly in place: candidates secured the recommendation of officials; they were impartially examined and ranked by the Ministry of Rites, and were appointed to office by the Ministry of Personnel so that selection and appointment were separated.

The procedures and safeguards, the various kinds of degrees including those obtainable by purchase or by simple recommendation, the struggles over content and vicissitudes of policy, the apportionment of degree quotas by administrative areas, the continuing "examination life" of an official, all these complexities make up an enormous record. Over the centuries in major provincial capitals thousands would compete triennially, as they do now every year. The elite thus created was hardly more than 2 percent of the population, about the same proportion as Chinese university graduates today. The tragedy of Mao's revolution is that in trying to shake off the elitist incubus of China's past he decried learning in general.

Unger and Shirk quote many first-person accounts. As the competition intensified in the 1960s among the increasing numbers of students, tension built up between the political activists, mainly in the Communist Youth League, and the academic achievers, mainly from nonproletarian families. Susan Shirk contrasts them as Virtuocracy versus Meritocracy. Ambitious students had to choose which route to follow. Activism injected one into politics, even precariously into power, but it alienated individuals from one another and, in the end, even from the political system. This was because the standards of correct political behavior were vague, subjective, and dangerously changeable; one was judged within one's peer group; and in political competition one advanced oneself by harming others.

Shirk concludes that within the Virtuocracy, "instead of cooperation there was intense individual competition, both academic and political. Students did not admire and confide in political activists, they avoided them. The regime's political demands on individuals strengthened rather than weakened friendship ties. Students kept their public criticism on a superficial level in order to protect their friends. Mutual criticism deteriorated into a superficial ritual . . . The effort . . . produced not the 'revolutionary successors' Mao had hoped for but wary adapters." Eventually in the Cultural Revolution "the penetration of politics into every corner of social and economic life destroyed people's trust of one another and of their leaders."

This failure of virtuocratic activism ("politics in command") in the schools lay behind the eventual student warfare during the Cultural Revolution. Jonathan Unger's tabulations of the affinities of his interviewees and their classmates as Red Guards show that "their factionalism was tantamount to class warfare": in Canton Mao's loyalist East Wind Red Guards were primarily red-class students; their rebel adversaries the Red Flag Red Guards were primarily of middle- and bad-class origin. Broader in scope than Shirk's, Unger's book recounts how, after the student warfare of 1967 had been quelled by the forcible rustication of the Red Guards, Maoist reforms took over China's education: key-point schools and entrance examinations were abolished in favor of a system of recommendation (the traditional alternative to examination), rural branch schools were set up to facilitate student labor in the fields, the curriculum was watered down, and academic achievement was positively discouraged.

After Mao died in 1976, all this had to be reversed. Liu Shao-ch'i has now been rehabilitated. Exams are back in. Education is forging ahead. But Mao's Great Revolution for a Proletarian Culture remains a nearly incredible cataclysm—appealing in aim perhaps, but appalling in detail and awesomely destructive. We are still far from understanding it. The 800 million peasants are still there in the villages. How are they to be educated for modern life?

22

Growing Up during the
Cultural Revolution

Son of the Revolution is actually three stories in one: first, a graphic I-was-there account of what it was like to grow up during the Cultural Revolution; second, a cliff-hanger love story with a happy ending; and third, a poignant analysis of how Chinese people have tried and failed, and tried again, to break out of their past. Each of these accounts is worth reading on its own.

By the time Liang Heng was born in 1954, the Chinese Communist Party had had its early success in reuniting the country, quelling inflation, beginning Soviet-style industrialization, and re-organizing the countryside. The old private plots were being combined in more efficient big fields under village production teams. To change both the land and the people, the Party had developed the technique of mass campaigns, mobilizing China's 600 million people to attack not only flood and drought but also the old evils of landlordism, capitalism, imperialism, or anything that seemed to have held China back. Many successes had been achieved. China had fought the Americans to a standstill in Korea. Mao and his colleagues, working as a team, had changed the world.

The first four words Liang Heng learns to speak are those for Papa, Mama, Grandma, and Chairman Mao. When at age three he climbs out of his crib at the boring day-care center and runs home to Grandma, he is punished for failing to be "Chairman Mao's

This review of Liang Heng and Judith Shapiro, *Son of the Revolution* (New York: Knopf, 1983), appeared as "Blind Obedience" in the *New York Review of Books*, May 12, 1983. Reprinted with permission from the *New York Review of Books*. Copyright © 1983 Nyrev, Inc.

good little boy." His father, a reporter on the *Hunan Daily* in Changsha, and his mother, a clerk in the Public Security Bureau, are both devout activists. They dream of "the day when they would be deemed pure and devoted enough to be accepted into the Party." But they never make it, for the revolution has to be fed with victims.

During the Hundred Flowers Campaign the mother is urged to voice criticisms. She finally succeeds in dutifully coming up with a mild critique of her supervisor. Suddenly in 1957 the Anti-Rightist Campaign erupts. Her bureau has a quota of Rightists to find and she is made a target, denounced, disgraced, and condemned, deprived of her cadre status and salary, and sent to the countryside for reform through labor. "There was no court of appeal. My naive and trusting mother went to work as a peasant."

This devastating ordeal ushers Liang Heng into a world of ideological politics, oppression, and injustice. His father and mother had married through the arrangement of friends. Working hard for the revolution, they had had little time together. "Father believed in the Party with his whole heart, believed that the Party could never make a mistake." In a vain effort to free his children from the Rightist taint, he denounces his wife and later divorces her. The mother feels horribly ashamed. When her brother protests, he is labeled a Rightist too. The son resents his mother's having wrecked their family life. He finds himself harassed and ostracized in primary school.

The boy grows up through three stages of experience as a Red Guard, a peasant, and a factory worker. By the time he is twelve in 1966, Chairman Mao sets off the Cultural Revolution. In July Mao swims in the Yangtze. In August he writes, "Bombard the headquarters." Liang Heng joins in and attacks his teachers only to find suddenly that his father, who has a brother in Taiwan, has been declared a Rightist and comes under attack himself. A work team demands that the son denounce his father; his father counsels him to do so. Big "struggle meetings" parade the miscreants and end up with public torture.

This terror against bureaucrats and intellectuals occurs in an atmosphere of tremendous enthusiasm and exultation over the triumph of virtue and the worship of Chairman Mao. Little Liang Heng puts on a Red Guard armband and walks with a group on his own Long March, 240 miles cross-country to the Jinggang Mountain, where Mao began his rebellion in 1928. The bands of youths making Long Marches are fanatically devoted to the great cause of making revolution. They reach the top of the mountain in rain and snow, exhausted and ill with severe diarrhea. As thousands of Long Marchers converge upon this shrine, they have to be evacuated to save their lives. Meningitis kills many after Liang's group have been taken out by army truck.

In 1966–1967 Liang Heng travels to Canton and to Peking with the hundreds of thousands of youths who are riding the trains free to explore their country. In Peking, as a Red Guard at age thirteen, he is set to guard a famous pianist who has treacherously won a prize in Moscow and is to be struggled with.

I was very proud . . . I stood with my hands at my waist, guarding him fiercely . . . Liu Shi-kun looked up . . . but I immediately barked, "Don't move," and he returned to his original position.

After a while, he licked his lips and half whispered, "Please give me some water. I'm thirsty."

I didn't know what to do. A Revolutionary shouldn't give water to his enemy, but I couldn't just stand there with water in the thermos only a few feet away. But what if someone saw me? . . . I quickly poured a cup from the thermos . . . As he drank it down I said fiercely, "You can't tell anyone about this, or next time I won't give you anything at all."

On May 1, 1967, Liang Heng goes with his group to the Summer Palace. Chairman Mao has departed. "All that remained of him was the touch of his hand on the hands of a few who had been lucky enough to get close to him . . . Those Chairman Mao had touched now became the focus of our fervor. Everyone surged toward them with outstretched arms in hopes of transferring the sacred touch to their own hands . . . shaking the hand of someone who had shaken hands with Our Great Saving Star . . . until sometimes handshakes were removed as much as one hundred times from the original one."

Back in Changsha in mid-1967 the Red Guard factions begin to use guns against one another. This produces civil war in the streets and violent deaths from gunfire even among comrades, since they do not know how to use firearms. By September Chairman Mao has to order the army in to stop the fighting and recover the guns. By early 1968 Liang Heng's two older sisters have been signed up to go down to the countryside and help the peasants. At the same time his father is sent to a Mao study class under military discipline in a barracks. At age fourteen Liang is alone in his family's house, living on a small part of his father's salary and consorting with other boys in gangs. They learn how to fight, drink, and steal, and become friends with hoodlums in a hand-to-mouth existence. Liang has already learned never to express an opinion on ideological matters. Now he finds out how to live without a family and fend for himself.

By the time he is fifteen in 1969, his father has been cleared and "liberated" to go to the country and be a peasant. Father and son go together. They give up their city residence cards and after a two-day journey find themselves in a production team in a remote village. The boy learns how to do farm work. The poverty amazes him. The farm couple he lives with share a single good pair of pants, worn by whichever one goes to market. They often eat the rice hulls issued by the government as pig feed. "Every time Old Guo took a pig to market, he fed it watered-down sop to bloat its belly and plugged its anus with cloth to keep it from losing precious poundage." In this medieval village, "less than a third of the people had even been to the town," only 4 miles away.

Eventually, as a cadre's son, Liang is able to go off to a middle school, three years after graduating from primary school. He gets a better supply of rice because of his father's status, but he is still the son of a Rightist, controlled and harassed by the students of peasant background. There are no books and little to study. With a gang he goes out at night to steal sweet potatoes from the fields, lying in the mud and eating them raw. Still, in the school storeroom he finds a cache of books that he can steal and secretly read. When he is brutally interrogated about a friend in Peking, who he later finds was in the ultraleftist May 16 group, his disillusion with the twists and turns of the revolution is complete. Kept out of upper middle school, he thinks of suicide. But his father has become an invalid, and Liang Heng nurses him in the village until in early 1971 the father is permitted to move back to a town, where he busies himself writing speeches for bureaucrats.

Thus at age seventeen Liang Heng is able to go to upper middle school. He is unusually tall—five feet eleven inches—and makes himself a basketball star, becoming team captain after his first year.

He goes in for training from 4 A.M. on and eats enormously, growing to six foot one. He is sent to an athletic training school and in the fall of 1972 plays in the provincial meet. Although a coach selects him for a factory team, he is disqualified because he is not a worker. His father refuses to permit Liang Heng to become a worker because he feels he should go to college, but he finally consents when this seems to be the only way forward. So Liang Heng becomes a worker in the shale-oil factory and plays basketball all over Hunan until he is invited to become a professional athlete. However, he cannot pass the political test, since he has an uncle still in Taiwan and his parents have been Rightists.

As a factory worker, he is amazed to find that no one works. Time is frittered away in daily rituals. Production is endlessly delayed by lack of supplies. He determines to pursue a secret reading program. His father, now forty-nine, has a stroke and must retire. By the time Chairman Mao dies in 1976, Liang Heng has spent two years as a peasant and four as a factory worker. He bestows gifts on the appropriate people to get himself nominated as a worker-peasant student to go to college from his factory, but then in 1977 national examinations are reinstituted. After two months' cramming he passes them, the only successful candidate from his factory, and is admitted to the Hunan Teachers' College for four years' training to become a teacher. It is February 1978. He is twenty-three years old, and when he receives this honor he gets inside an automobile for the first time. Except for actually being a soldier, he has tasted the major experiences open to his generation. He has kept in touch with his scattered family. His sisters are now married in the countryside. In the absence of family life, he has survived without the Party's becoming his foster parent. He knows how to work hard and to give presents to his superiors so as to get through the back door. He can keep his own counsel. Most of all, he has kept the self-image of an intellectual.

The love story that is a major attraction of *Son of the Revolution* begins with Liang Heng's frustrating relations with young women. One in Canton he corresponds with and eventually goes to see, but her father suspects his Rightist background and righteously warns him off. The girl is simply terrified. Another young woman he meets on a train. Sympathizing with her domestic problems, he makes another trip to Canton and impersonates a high cadre in order to browbeat her stepbrother, who is trying to force her actual brother to go in his place to the countryside. Finally, on a train to Shanghai he meets a woman conductor who is trying to help another woman wrongly accused. Liang Heng responds to people of such generosity and soon is having an affair with this young woman, who proves to be the daughter of a high military commander, former head of public security in Hunan. When she finally introduces Liang Heng to her family in their posh house, the father is cordiality itself but later berates his daughter fiercely for thinking of marrying below her station. He proceeds to whip her to enforce his point. The love affair dies.

At the Hunan Teachers' College dances are occasionally held, but their political propriety is questioned. The boys find it safer to dance with each other. Suddenly in the spring of 1979, "I heard that the new American teacher in the Foreign Languages Department was scheduled to perform some dances . . . This was the first chance I had ever had to see one of those high-nosed, big-eyed creatures in person . . . She seemed so relaxed and yet so skilled, very different from the Chinese women dancers, who controlled their bodies tightly . . . This Western dance was so pleasant to watch in its immeasurable freedom!" The next fall, when he has to write an English paper, it is suggested he go see this American teacher to get it corrected. "I asked my best friend to go to her home with me, and he was shocked. People might suspect us of all kinds of things if we sought out a foreigner! But when I said I would go without him, he insisted on coming along, for my sake. If I were questioned, he could bear witness to the innocence of what had been said and done."

They go, and the teacher lends him books and agrees to find time to discuss literature. When he goes alone to see her again, he finds that her conversation ranges over literature, education, and aesthetics. "I thought it astonishing that a girl of only twenty-five should be so well educated . . . I was also deeply impressed by the fact that she never asked me about my political background . . . Our friendship grew quickly, . . . and I began to understand that she, too, was lonely, for although the teachers and students treated her warmly, . . . no one dared to be her real friend . . . Instinctively,

I knew that if I could make her understand me, I would win her. So I shared my past with her in great detail, omitting nothing. She was so moved by my story that she wrote it all down, evening after evening . . . I felt her feelings and respect growing, and at the same time my wounds seemed gradually to dry up and heal."

Judith Shapiro was born in New York in 1953. She went to the Brearley School and graduated from Princeton in 1975 in anthropology with a beginning course in Chinese, which she continued at Columbia and the China Institute in New York. In 1977 she took an M.A. in comparative literature at the University of Illinois and then made her first trip to China. In 1979 she took an M.A. in Asian studies at Berkeley before accepting the post of teacher at Changsha. After eight years' study of Chinese she was fascinated by the opening up of contact and the opportunity to understand the revolution. After their first long conversation she told Liang Heng that "she had learned more about China from me in one evening than in her previous six months there." They soon felt that their whole lives had brought them together.

Fearing discovery, they tell the responsible cadre that they propose to marry. But even though marriage between Chinese and foreigners is now permitted, the college authorities counsel against it. "Remember that you are Chinese," they say sternly to Liang. "You must love your motherland. There is a difference between insiders and outsiders." They say they will ask his parents for their opinions. This precipitates a crisis: Liang Heng rushes with Judy to see his mother and subsequently his father, lest they be persuaded to withhold their permission. The authorities continue to drag their feet. The dean takes the position that since students are not allowed to marry, Liang Heng will have to drop out of college.

Finally Judy appeals directly to the top man in China, Deng Xiaoping at the Central Committee in Peking. "It seemed incredible then—and still seems so now—but Deng, the most powerful man in the country, read Judy's appeal. An official later told me privately that he frowned impatiently, said, 'Of course they should be allowed to marry,' and scrawled instructions." Their aggressive bravado pulls it off. Eventually they go back to New York, where Liang Heng is now studying for a Ph.D. at Columbia, while Judy Shapiro is an interpreter for the State Department, guiding delegations to and from China.

•   •   •

The success of *Son of the Revolution* hinges on the fact that while the life is that of Liang Heng, the writer is Judy Shapiro. The words are hers: he is her informant. Producing a book like this takes far more intimate and prolonged collaboration than producing a baby, and the happy couple are to be congratulated. Translation from languages as distant as Chinese or Japanese is, of course, a two-stage operation. The original writing must be thoroughly grasped, but to "translate" it requires creating a new work in English. In this case the notes and recollections were in Chinese, but the story was worked out and conversation dubbed in by the authors together. Both of them are devoted to the cause of the Chinese people but thoroughly aware of the ideological pitfalls into which their leaders have fallen and the unpleasantness of many realities in the People's Republic that must be faced.

Readers will draw the conclusions they prefer from the realistic touches of this first-person story. A distant nonpeasant like myself may be struck with the way people persist in their social roles. One declared aim of Mao's revolution was to break down the special status of intellectuals, who had for so long been manufactured and coopted by imperial dynasties through their official examinations. Learning in the old days had been a tool of power, the key to indoctrination and the maintenance of orthodoxy. The notorious victimization of intellectuals during the Cultural Revolution expressed Mao's contempt for them as "parasites," an idea that was completely out of date, whatever validity it may once have had. The real evil Mao faced was the unrestrained autocracy of the official class, the new Party bureaucrats, and the authoritarian habits of mind they displayed and inculcated in others.

Son of the Revolution's worm's-eye view of the meeting of intellectuals and peasants shows us what Mao was up against. Both the peasants and the intellectuals were political followers. Neither had any sanction in mind that would give them an ideological basis for disagreeing with the authorities. Liang Heng's father had broad literary interests and "was an accomplished poet as well as an amateur composer and conductor," but his devotion to the Party enslaved his mind. The more he was kicked around the less he attempted to make an independent judgment. His being an intellectual was combined with an utter passivity in politics. When activists unjustly accuse his wife, instead of denouncing them and defending her, he denounces and finally divorces her in order to placate them. He is eager to do to himself and to others whatever the Party asks. He goes through prolonged criticism and ideological reconditioning in order to lose his class character and achieve a proletarian view. Yet when he is finally sent down to the production team in the countryside, the father finds that he is still a literatus and teacher and that the peasants are still peasants ready to take his instruction. He blows his whistle at dawn to get the peasants to a meeting for Mao slogans. He becomes the local cadre who explains the dictates of the Party from above.

His faith in the Party is diminished only in 1969 when the Party zealots in the city become determined to "cut off the tail of capitalism" in the countryside. They demand that all private raising of pigs, chickens, and ducks be abandoned lest it preserve the evil tendencies of capitalism among the peasantry. In Liang's production team this means a destruction of sideline income, which will bring malnutrition, maybe starvation. One bold farmer meets the cadre from outside with the statement that his ducks are being prepared for Chairman Mao and he will send them to Peking. "Whoever is crazy enough to try to kill my ducks, well, he's the one opposing Chairman Mao!" The cadre goes off discomfited, but Liang's father dutifully persuades the farmer to kill his ducklings. Yet for the first time he does not actually defend the Party's policy. His devotion has been used up.

Liang's father seems to embody China's problem. He is so persistent in being an intellectual, so subservient to authority. He cannot conceive any sanction for standing up against the dictates of the Party. But the state power, formerly superficial and unobtrusive in the village, now reaches through the Party to affect even the villager's ducklings. How is the state power to be limited and the ducks protected?

Liang and Shapiro have only one overt message to convey and that is gently put: as he prepares to leave China for study abroad, Liang Heng realizes "how deeply I loved my motherland and her people . . . By experiencing disaster my generation did learn one terribly important thing—the danger that lies in blind obedience."

PART FIVE

Fallout: America's Disillusioned Optimism

The resumption of Chinese-American relations in 1979 sparked a syndrome of enthusiasm and disillusionment characterized by our euphoria when Vice Premier Deng Xiaoping toured the United States and wore a ten-gallon hat while riding in a Texas stagecoach, whereupon he returned to China and suddenly attacked the Vietnamese in a border war of Chinese-style chastisement.

Since the story is far from over, one can only comment that the two motifs of admiration and fear have not disappeared. China's open door to the outside world of trade and investment under Deng Xiaoping calls forth our approval, yet a closer look shows that Chinese life is fraught with endemic evils quite counter to the tenets of liberalism, to say nothing of that radical throwback, American conservatism. The pioneer American journalists who have tried to do investigative reporting return from Peking frustrated and disenchanted. They attempt to give us the real facts of Chinese life, yet our increased contact of the 1980s tends as usual to build up the old American feelings about China—the curious appeals of tourism, the hope of big business deals, the respect for the character of Chinese friends and for the intelligence of individual Chinese. For the moment we fall into a mood of disillusioned optimism: China suffers from many evils, but it is a country we can get along with.

23

Uncovering the Evils of the
Cultural Revolution

Chinese Shadows is a brilliant polemic that in 1974, as *Ombres chinoises*, blew the whistle on French adulation of Mao. Simon Leys is really Pierre Ryckmans, a Belgian art historian who has published several works of sinology—notably *Su Renshan: Rebel Painter and Madman in Nineteenth-Century China*, an anthology of *tzu*, or *poemes à chanter*, and a French translation, with commentaries, of the classic *Sun Tzu's Art of War*. Leys first visited China in 1955, penetrated Chinese life in the most efficacious way by marrying a Chinese woman (his book is dedicated to her), and lived for five years in Hong Kong. In 1971 he published *Les habits neufs du Président Mao* (Chairman Mao's new clothes), one of the most caustic exposés by a sinologist of the Cultural Revolution's basically anti-intellectual attack on China's cultural heritage.

In 1972 Leys spent six months in China, living in the Peking Hotel and taking seven trips into the provinces. He visited many of the cities and sites on the regular tour routes around Peking, the ancient capitals Loyang and Sian, the Linhsien irrigation project in Honan, the model Tachai Brigade in Shansi, Mao's Hunan birthplace, and Soochow and Hangchow near Shanghai. *Chinese Shadows* was written mainly in 1972 and 1973. Leys got to China again briefly in the latter year, and a few notes were added as of 1976. Thus Leys has seen as much as most observers. He excels them in knowledge and vigor of expression.

The autopsy on Mao has long since downgraded his economics,

This review of Simon Leys, *Chinese Shadows* (New York: Viking Press, 1977), appeared as "Mao's War on Culture" in the *New York Times Book Review,* August 28, 1977. Copyright © 1977 by the New York Times Company. Reprinted by permission.

and the Soviets are still enraged over his politics—they are against teenage Red Guards attacking party bureaucrats. But of all the eggs Mao broke to make his revolutionary omelet, the Western public has been most concerned over the fate of China's culture and her intellectuals. *Chinese Shadows* denounces the attack on them in Mao's Cultural Revolution. The book thus shows the gulf separating Western liberals and Maoist bureaucrats; and since neither tribe is likely to disappear, their differences deserve attention.

They differ first on the role of the scholar. For thirteen hundred years, until 1905, Chinese scholars were self-indoctrinated, by competing in the labyrinthine examination system, to become docile supporters of the regime. A modern intelligentsia of critics, reformers, and revolutionaries has flourished only in the present century, and Mao, the peasant organizer, never admired or trusted their independence of mind and spirit. For him they still symbolized the specially privileged arrogance of the old scholar-official ruling class. His very capacity to commune with peasant villagers made Mao both anti-intellectual and anti-aesthetic. Like so many touchy emperors intent on power, he terrorized and stultified writers and artists, as did his wife, Chiang Ch'ing, until she was put away.

Simon Leys is in the almost equally venerable tradition of outsiders who fall under the spell of Chinese culture, become entranced with its beauties, and find themselves enlarged as they grow to appreciate it. Such involvement leads inevitably to a certain possessiveness on the part of these foreigners, whose marginal and always limited experience of China bulks so large in their own lives. They sympathize with their Chinese counterparts, resent bureaucratic callousness toward the arts and letters, and sometimes offer Western-style criticisms that in Chinese politics would constitute traitorous defiance of the regime.

Leys begins *Chinese Shadows* by debunking Chinese tourism— its limitation to a dozen cities, its confinement within them to grand hotels and limousines, the forging of a "friendship between peoples" that prevents friendship between persons. "Out of eight hundred million Chinese, foreigners meet about sixty individuals . . . for whom greeting foreigners is a full-time job." He sees the special privileges that separate foreigners from the Chinese people as "a shameful legacy of the old imperialist-colonialist epoch." He derides the "docile visitors" who never ride a bus with Chinese people or eat noodles at a street stand but "meekly accept their cloistered existence in dismal palaces, blind and deaf to Chinese sights and sounds." Since these "travelers know nothing, nothing surprises them"—not the Number Two man of many years (Liu Shao-ch'i) suddenly becoming a traitor, nor Mao's longtime confidential secretary (Chen Po-ta) turning out to be a crook, nor his second heir designate and "closest comrade-in-arms" (Lin Piao) unexpectedly trying to assassinate him. Leys also depicts the unfavored foreigners—both the correspondents, who are harassed as spies, and the diplomats in their ghettos. "Travelers . . . are less conscious that they are being carried everywhere in a cage; the residents, who must stay put in Peking, have plenty of time to count all the bars."

Other chapters deal with the superficiality of the guided tours, taking a few swipes at the phony heroes and the party-line philosophizing, and then with the class struggle, the bureaucracy, and the universities. Traveling rather widely in the aftermath of the Cultural Revolution, Leys was extremely sensitive to the scars it had left. The two writers he quotes repeatedly are Lu Hsun, the great political satirist of the 1920s and 1930s, and George Orwell. In the People's Republic he sees totalitarianism at work—a "Maoist cancer . . . gnawing away at the face of China . . . This gigantic enterprise of cretinizing the most intelligent people on earth . . . twenty years of systematic training in aggression, of legitimizing violence and hatred. The daily witnessing of looting, revenge, cruelties, humiliations inflicted by children on their elders under the pretext of 'class struggle'; the obligation to be present at, if not take an active part in, the public denunciation of neighbors, friends, fellow workers and parents." Much of this stems from Mao's 1942 talks on arts and letters at Yenan, a "clearly expressed resolution to destroy critical intelligence . . . [a] war against the mind [which] has resulted in the near total extinction of Chinese intellectuals *as such.*"

Without its city walls and gates and the memorial arches that once spanned the main streets, Peking is, as Leys sees it, "a murdered town, a disfigured ghost of what was once one of the most beautiful cities in the world." The martyrs' memorial in the middle of the great new Tien-an Men Square symbolizes "the Maoist rape of the ancient capital . . . this insignificant granitic phallus receives all its enormous significance from the blasphemous stupidity of its location," breaking the harmony between the Tien-an Men and Peking's front gate. The monument is a "revolutionary-proletarian obscenity." (This is the view of an architect concerned about aesthetic tradition, not that of a Chinese revolutionary concerned about honoring fallen comrades.) Meanwhile, the general destruction or neglect of ancient temples and other monuments, except for a couple of showplaces in each principal city, was concealed from the outside world by sending abroad the brilliant exhibit of "archeological treasures unearthed during the Cultural Revolution."

Mao's peasant dislike of scholarship appeared most clearly in the closing down of higher education for almost five years (surely a modern world record). Professors were harassed, vilified, and relegated to manual labor; but their proletarian replacements proved to have little to offer and, after being reeducated by using their muscles, nine-tenths of the old teaching staff reappeared, though they now lacked authority among the students. Meanwhile, books and periodicals, except for Mao's works, were no longer published. "All movies, plays, and operas from before the Cultural Revolution disappeared . . . A good number of writers, artists, and intellectuals committed suicide." After these excesses, recovery was pathetically slow and hesitant: "The Chinese people remain thirsty for culture." *Chinese Shadows* thus explains the genuine rejoicing that greeted the fall of Mao's epigones, the Gang of Four, in October of 1979.

Leys accounts for this tragic story of anti-intellectualism only in the pessimistic terms used by Orwell and Lu Hsun. He sees the "monolithic orthodoxy" of the Ming despotism perpetuated by the Ch'ing. Some historians would go further and see China's earlier and freer cultural development "derailed" ever since the Mongol conquest. At any rate, since the Chinese Revolution was bigger than Mao, its excesses must be ascribed to the vindictiveness of peasants against the ruling class accumulated over the centuries. Once in power in this self-contained society, peasants, as always before, found little alternative to practicing the bureaucratism of their late class enemies and thus becoming a new ruling class. After all, Mao's Cultural Revolution was directed specifically against the old ruling class—its old ideas, old habits, old customs. Yet his belief that politics should dominate the arts and letters could have come straight from the Chien-lung emperor of the eighteenth century, who destroyed the entire families of writers who disparaged his dynasty.

This suggests that China's breaking out of bureaucratism (and the corruption that lies in wait for it whenever morale declines) will depend partly on a continuance of the kind of Chinese contact with the outer world that helped originally to fragment the old ruling class by creating a modern intelligentsia of independent entrepreneurs, industrialists, journalists, writers, artists, scientists, and even college professors. Such contact, of course, is now under way on a large scale.

It must also be said, to the detriment of Leys's case, that *Chinese Shadows* manages almost entirely to ignore the material achievements of the People's Republic—rebuilding the country with trees, dams, ditches, pumps, fields, crops, and factories; remaking the society with literacy, organization, technical skills, public health, political participation, patriotism, hard work, cooperation and self-respect. If Chou En-lai were still alive to explain it all to foreigners, he might point out that revolutions zig and zag. He would not be pessimistic, and neither should we. China is not Russia, and the Chinese style of party autocracy is not just a copy of the Soviet style. On the contrary, it has deep roots in China's so-called legalist tradition, which Mao invoked. Perhaps today Leys would see more chance that the alternative Confucian tradition of individual self-cultivation may still ameliorate China's future.

24

The Now-It-Can-Be-Told Reports
of Journalists

Our relations with China are notoriously subject to swings of opinion. Idealization and disillusion, euphoria and cynicism follow each other as though our national psychology were regulated by some manic-depressive clock. The current trend toward disillusionment about the quality of life in China is no doubt part of a cycle, swinging back from the overblown enthusiasm of the early Maoist revolution of the 1950s. But the new disillusion may also represent a new fact of life, that the Chinese people are in an unprecedented quagmire created by history as well as by the Maoist revolution. Since their hard fate affects ours, it is a time for understanding and for thinking twice. Disillusion could become a reciprocal process.

• • •

In the summer of 1943, when wartime propaganda and censorship had built up in the United States a better-than-life image of Chiang Kai-shek's Free China, three writers whose names began with B— Pearl Buck, Hanson Baldwin, and T. A. Bisson—punctured the rosy-hued balloon by reporting Kuomintang China's actual fatigue, corruption, demoralization, and disunity. The "three Bs," though denounced in Chungking as saboteurs, struck a blow for

This chapter is based on a review of Fox Butterfield, *China: Alive in the Bitter Sea* (New York: Times Books, 1982), and of Richard Bernstein, *From the Center of the Earth: The Search for the Truth about China* (Boston: Little, Brown, 1982), that appeared in the *New York Review of Books,* May 27, 1982, and on a review of Jay Mathews and Linda Mathews, *One Billion: A China Chronicle* (New York: Random House, 1983), that appeared in the *New York Review of Books,* January 19, 1984. Reprinted with permission from the *New York Review of Books.* Copyright © 1982, 1984 Nyrev, Inc.

realism: they asked Americans to face the reality of China's problems, while Chiang Kai-shek told his officials to see less of Americans. Now come two more Bs—Fox Butterfield and Richard Bernstein—also asking us to face unpleasant facts.

Again, as forty years ago, we are caught in the Sino-American culture gap. Muckraking, now called investigative reporting, is a public service to Americans, who need their daily muck to feel healthily democratic. But it is seen as an unfriendly if not treasonous disservice to the established order in China, which has normally maintained itself partly by looking good. Since both the United States and China seem to be becoming less governable, no matter what ideologies they cling to, the shortfall in China between ideal and real is poignant news in America, whereas to have it talked about may be considered bad news by the government in China. Yet Peking is committed to "seek truth from facts." We all confront the usual problem, What is true, on balance?

Butterfield and Bernstein both start by examining the special status accorded foreigners in China and the journalist's need to break out of the polite cocoon of interesting bus trips and succulent dinners that makes tourism to China such a success. Both reporters have the special merit of being academically trained sinologists and historians, as well as first-rate journalists. Unlike travelers disoriented by culture shock, they can share the Chinese habit of viewing the present against the long sweep of the past.

They also represent the first wave of Chinese-speaking American correspondents to be stationed in Peking after the normalization of 1979. By that time modern-minded victims of Mao's decade of Cultural Revolution (1966–1976) at last felt free to tell their stories of mindless victimization by adolescent Red Guards and Maoists. Both authors report case histories with names changed and identities masked, but the horror stories are in tune with much recent reporting. Most appalling is the way patriotic Chinese in the United States who went back to help build a new China were eventually suspected, accused, condemned, imprisoned, and put out of action because of their "bourgeois" (American) taint.

Fox Butterfield sets forth a vast amount of hard-won detail on the current regime and society. He began his Chinese studies in 1958 and went on to work for his Ph.D., partly in Taiwan. There, in 1969, he became a stringer for the *New York Times* and then spent ten years learning to be its top correspondent on China before opening its Peking bureau in 1979. Butterfield's self-assurance and attractiveness during twenty months in Peking helped him to accumulate data and personal testimony in meticulous detail. *Alive in the Bitter Sea (Ku-hai yu-sheng)* is a Buddhist adage about survival in suffering. Different chapters deal with the complex hierarchies of rank and special privilege, the use of personal connections to get ahead or even get along in the world, the social and circumstantial constraints on love and marriage, homelessness among young people, lack of incentives and efficiency in industry, the control of information, and a great deal more. It is the most comprehensive report available.

Richard Bernstein had seven years of basic training in Chinese Studies (1966–1973) before joining *Time* and reporting from Hong Kong and the mainland. His thoughtful essays make a shorter book, but an eloquent and perceptive one. His explorations of life, especially in Szechwan and in Peking, are laced with people and incidents, usually viewed in historical context. The daily lives of individual Chinese he finds drab, dull, and woefully restricted. Every time he went to look at the Great Wall, says Bernstein, he thought of the labor that originally went into it. When the First Emperor built it twenty-two hundred years ago, he threw China's abundant manpower at the problem of defense, much as we Americans today throw money at ours. So in 1958 Chairman Mao, who admired the First Emperor, attacked the problem of industrialization by also throwing China's manpower at it. He had mixed results.

Both books reflect the current Chinese backlash against the disaster of Mao's last decade. The great helmsman steered China backward and onto the rocks. Mao in his seventies had a nostalgic yen for the simplicity of his years in Yenan. He really hated bureaucrats and intellectuals. In the 1960s, when China, like the United States today, badly needed more constructive and better government, not less, Mao's version of "get the government off our backs" was to "bombard the headquarters" and "drag out the capitalist-roaders." In the turmoil created by the fanatical Red Guards, who felt themselves to be morally in the majority, some aspects of administration even ground to a halt.

No one called it Maoconomics, but the great helmsman's guerrilla mentality had some Reaganomic overtones. His distrust of central administration led him, for example, to flout the economic law of comparative advantage. Instead of having some provinces produce China's cotton and others China's rice, Mao wanted all provinces to be potential guerrilla bases, self-sufficient in food supply. As a result, production of cotton and rice declined. He also broke up the central statistical service and gave its functions back to the provinces, creating a statistical shambles. Mao's atavism, to be sure, was less amiable than Mr. Reagan's. He also had no way to surrender power.

Disillusion with Mao, which these reporters pass on to us from the Chinese scene, seems to be only the top layer of something more fundamental. Behind the fanatical destructiveness of Mao's revolution gone astray in the late 1960s, there lies a deeper problem that the Chinese people now have to live with: in sociological terms, the authoritarian state has taken over the society. Before this century Chinese governments tried primarily to stay in power and so maintained themselves by a combination of indoctrination, surveillance, and intimidation. But in the old days this was largely at the superficial level of the official establishment. It left the peasant masses in the villages under the leadership of the big extended families, the local elite. There was a rough balance between the centralized despotism of the ruling dynasty at Peking and the dispersed village communities held together by the dutiful bonds of the Confucian family system. From official life one could escape into the rural scene.

Modern times have seen this central/local balance destroyed. Rule by a dynastic family has given way to party dictatorship, which has brought modernized indoctrination, surveillance, and intimidation into every village and every urban family. Partly through telecommunications the peasant masses mobilized for revolution have been manipulated in political movements from the top down faster than means could be found to represent them from the bottom up. Mao's mass line, that the party must listen to the people, was still based on paternal authoritarianism. The officials still knew best. For instance, they would not arrest you unless they already knew you were guilty. When the able Canadian reporter John Burns was arrested by the agents in the car that always followed his, the Peking police at headquarters said to him, "Why are you here? Think it over and tell us." After several hours alone in detention he worked it out. "I looked at a map while driving and so took my eyes off the road, contrary to regulations." "That's right," they said. "Now you may go."

Butterfield describes the pervasive control system maintained at the three levels of work unit, street committee, and discussion group. The work unit dominates the individual as fully as the old family system ever could. It arranges food and clothing rations, housing, marriage, schooling, medical service, and recreation. It also controls correspondence and travel, while the street committee watches all behavior and contact, searches living quarters at will, and monitors marital relations to stop quarrels and unauthorized pregnancies. You can find privacy best by walking through a crowd. Meanwhile, your particular work is assigned you for the rest of your working life. Transfer to different work is difficult; and husbands and wives may be assigned to different cities. All wives work as well as housekeep. You express yourself freely only to one other person at a time, not if a third person is present; for the testimony of two witnesses can convict you of treasonous dissent. This is an unprecedented degree of collectivism such as the Chinese people have not experienced before.

The penetration of China's body politic by the old official despotism in a more intensive form has been compounded by a second great new fact: the appalling overcrowding of daily life by a doubling of the population since 1949. The material progress owing to electric water pumps, better seeds, afforestation, combining strip fields into bigger ones, bringing literacy and public health to the villages, and so on—all so promising in the 1950s—has all been eaten up by the disastrous increase of numbers. Many onetime economies of the revolution have been achieved, but overpopulation now imprisons the entire people in an inescapable competition to grab one's own bit of turf and security. People are mean to one another. Inadequate housing condemns them to more crowded living than ever before. A room of one's own is impossible. Marriage may be postponed because of lack of living space for another couple. The modern revolution in sexual self-expression is sadly inhibited. Standing in line to shop wastes hours every day. Having too many people on every job destroys the work ethic. People pollution reduces productivity per person and leaves the country condemned to poverty.

This crowding has intensified the evils of bureaucratism and favoritism. The Cultural Revolution left the Communist Party swollen with poorly educated people who joined up as opportunists and careerists, not warriors, and now they clutter the administration as incompetent timeservers. Mao's crusade created exactly what he feared—a regime of cynical bureaucrats jealous of their special privileges. More than ever, one gets ahead in China through personal connections, going through the back door. Self-serving sycophancy and corruption go hand in hand because success is measured not in money but in perquisites of housing, transportation, servants, special stores, and special schooling.

What perspectives can offset this disillusioned view? We know that peasant life generally has been a brutal *sauve qui peut*. Conditions in the countryside may be better than they used to be, and still be brutal for urban intellectuals sent down to the villages. Again, we know that early industrialization with its pollution, city growth, and labor exploitation has been a grim time for most peoples. Mao's revolution by its very success in bringing literacy and telecommunications to the great mass of people has roused hopes and expectations not easily fulfilled. Moreover, revolutions naturally exhaust themselves. It is thirty-seven years since Mao came to power. And, too, Butterfield and Bernstein found their friends and informants chiefly among city intellectuals, the group most likely to be distressed. Generalizing about a billion people involves many caveats. Yet the disillusion, stress, and unhappiness among educated Chinese come through in these books as facts seen and felt at first hand, part of a widespread mood that cannot be exorcised simply by understanding its causes.

China's mood has close practical implications for us. It can affect American policy and our relations. For Americans who espouse human rights as a secular religion, China has always presented a major problem. For a century, from 1844 to 1943, we enjoyed the privileges of the British-devised unequal treaties, which gave Americans in China the protection of American law. This extraterritoriality, now regarded in China as simple imperialism, must be recognized in retrospect as an American demand to enjoy in China our own type of civil liberties—legal rights to personal freedom, property holding, and self-expression even by missionaries—which represented the liberal creed.

The current picture of the Chinese state and society dominating the individual highlights China's lack of such a legal-liberal tradition. Chinese victimized by Mao's revolution could not appeal to a sanction higher than the moral judgment of the masses allegedly represented by the party organizers. The whole Chinese educated elite could thus be targeted as oppressors hated by Mao and his followers, partly, I suggest, because in time past the examination system had associated the educated with the rulers. Thus Mao's class struggle, once unleashed, could set out like a *jacquerie* to destroy the very people most needed to bring China into the modern world.

Before we conclude that we face a struggle between American and Chinese systems of social order, let us remember, as our missionaries learned during the century of treaty privileges in China, that good and bad are scattered about in both societies, and neither one has a monopoly of rectitude, sense, or efficiency. Today's leader, Deng Xiaoping, was intended to be a principal victim of the Cultural Revolution and is now a principal survivor. We can expect Mr. Deng and his managerial colleagues to take constructive steps and mount reform programs just as Confucian reformers did repeatedly in the old days.

Meanwhile we have had helmsman trouble ourselves. If by downgrading our esteem for the People's Republic we seem to condone Mr. Reagan's early campaign rhetoric about upgrading relations with Taiwan, we can create trouble no one needs. At present the Deng Xiaoping regime sees the great need for intellectual skills such as exchanges with America can provide. Butterfield and Bernstein met many Chinese eager to escape abroad from the boring comformity of Chinese life. But the American example conveyed by television and by word of mouth can inspire both discontent with Chinese life and a backlash against America. We could, with our usual inadvertence, fill again the role of national enemy. Mao's activation in politics of formerly inert rural masses roused an anti-intellectual, antiforeign fanaticism that still lies somewhere below the surface. Peking has to steer its course with one eye on the mass of people and party activists who were taught from childhood to see America as the great imperialist enemy.

Perhaps the most irksome thought to the Chinese patriot today is the realization that under Mao the Chinese people did stand up, free to make their own revolution, and then brought disaster upon themselves. This is humiliating. Blaming the Gang of Four is of course a fig leaf. The Chinese people followed Mao, and Mao blew it. But as with all great men, it will appear in time that Mao led by keeping out in front of his followers. They are left to confront the paradox: China was great, now it is poor. Why? Who was the culprit?

In these circumstances we can draw at least one conclusion. For Mr. Reagan to "upgrade" Taiwan and undo the Nixon-Carter normalization, which set up official relations only with Peking and only unofficial relations with Taiwan, would play into the hands of Deng Xiaoping's latent opposition. Taiwan is doing well, not damaged by Carter's normalization with Peking. The regime there of course acclaims Mr. Reagan's out-of-date sentiments and claims still to be the "sovereign Republic of China," still defiant in the civil war that ended in fact in 1949. It conducts a wide-ranging public relations campaign focused especially on American state and city leaders. Delegations, paid guests, conferences, and official visits build bonds of friendship. More than seventeen thousand students come to the United States from Taiwan yearly, compared with half that number from the PRC. We try to be friends with all Chinese and enjoy, sometimes naively, our warm relations with the People's Republic as well as with Taiwan. But Taiwan's inside track with Reaganite Republicans inspires a Peking counterattack. It is not at all strange that Peking feels it has to make an issue of our arming Taiwan.

These trends, if not halted, could unexpectedly produce big disillusionment on both sides, mutual and reciprocal. If life in China has become as grim as Butterfield and Bernstein tell us, we should watch our step. China's masses are not necessarily rational and may be a sleeping monster. And that may be precisely how they feel about us, too.

How can we forestall this ominous possibility?

•   •   •

The resolution of Chinese-American problems by means of friendly contact is suggested by a journalist family reporting from Peking. In Jay and Linda Mathews' *One Billion: A China Chronicle* the sympathetic yet critical balance of attitude no doubt reflects the authors' experience living together in China. Linda Mathews was the first female editor of the *Harvard Crimson* and went on to take a law degree before eventually becoming Peking bureau chief for the *Los Angeles Times*. Jay Mathews was also a journalist on the *Crimson* but went into Chinese studies and took an M.A. before joining the *Washington Post* and eventually becoming its Peking bureau chief. When the pair married and had two children, they mixed collaboration and competition. By living in China as a family, they were in an unusual position to explore nooks and crannies of the society around them.

The humane balance of their approach is evident first of all in the structure of the book, which is really a journalists' effort (the best I know) to capture that elusive but ubiquitous entity known as "Chinese culture," or what makes the Chinese tick. The book's first part stresses the collective sense that forms the matrix of Chinese behavior, the personal connections (*kuan-hsi*) by which things are accomplished. "Being Chinese . . . is a commitment to one another—billions of small relationships becoming one great whole." Next, the authors write of the pervasive sense of history, a different and quite un-American perspective on the present day. Finally, they explain how individuals are identified by their relationships, primarily their work units, today's distillation of the Confucian five relationships that used to tie people to their families.

The three parts of the book deal first with what the authors call "One Billion," the crowded life of the people, then with "The System," which organizes their lives, and finally with "Escape," the leisure arts that help them to survive the system. This organization allows the Mathewses to discuss the daily experience of many city people; but they were able to talk to only a few rather well-off country people. They record many conversations and many case histories. In a chapter called "Working," they show the continual difficulty of incentives under socialism; "Language" shows the effort at reform of writing in order to make it more efficient. In the chapter on sex, the absence of privacy and knowledge is typified by girls who worry that kissing may make them pregnant. The revolution, they write, "stopped at the bedroom door." In this matter China has a long way to go. Meanwhile, marriage itself continues to be a very secure institution, carefully planned and practically sustained. On the other hand, the Chinese specialty of having children confronts the new law: "One is enough," say the billboards in Peking. To the Chinese, this is the curse hanging over their pride at being the world's only billion-member nation.

The chapters concerned with "the system" show how the Chinese manage to circumvent it, largely by way of the back door, with gifts in hand. Information is a government monopoly, but the 9 million restricted copies of *Reference News,* by quoting the foreign press, can bounce "signals back to the Chinese people." The examination system has come back with a vengeance: 5 million young people may take the nationwide exams, and one in twenty of these applicants may get into college. A college population of 2 million (not yet attained) would be 0.2 percent of the population. The highly educated are as tiny an elite as ever. The perquisites of the highly placed are opulent.

The Mathewses show how sensitive the authorities are to dissent. The government needs the intellectuals' support and will, they believe, have to move carefully when limiting intellectual freedoms. But "The Law" is as Draconian as ever, weeding out malefactors with a bullet in the brain. "The whole province [of Ch'inghai, northeast of Tibet] is a sort of prison colony." Penal labor camps give the government, in the Soviet style, "a reliable supply of low-cost labor which can be moved about the country at will." The new legal system is far from catching up with injustice.

The final part, "Escape," suggests a synthesis: the overcrowding, bureaucratization, and police dictatorship are moderated not only by the Chinese cuisine, by the theater and graphic arts, by movies, music, and literature, but by "fun and games," including cricket-fighting, gambling, betting, sports, and other diversions. The authors also recount jokes from the fast satiric stage dialogues (*hsiang-sheng*), another Chinese specialty. Three prisoners explain to one another how they got in jail: "I am here because I supported Deng Xiaoping," says one. "I am here because I opposed Deng Xiaoping," says the second. Says the third, "I am here because I *am* Deng Xiaoping."

The Mathewses report "a daily struggle between a popular

yearning to grasp material incentives and democracy, and stubborn resistance from an officeholding class stiffened by centuries of experience in holding on to power." They see the Chinese poised on the "edge of political unrest . . . collapse . . . despair . . . their pride and confidence . . . at a critical point." Yet they know how to survive the system. The Chinese "resent—some actively, the majority almost unconsciously—the oppression and inconvenience of their form of government but prefer to finesse it rather than challenge it outright."

In short, they live with the revived bureaucratic state on their backs. It is sanctioned by the national collective spirit and clamped on by modern technology. In this fix the Chinese practice what we may call a private mini-individualism that consists in freedom in small things that are beneath collective concern. The Western faith in legally protected public individualism, currently expressed in our concern for human rights, probably appeals to the highly educated Chinese elite more than Christianity ever did. But even they for now have to put the collective national interest ahead of individual rights. As in this country we try to defend ourselves against the computer, we can feel we have something in common with the Chinese.

25

We Still Confront Two Chinas

As we enjoy the Chinese-American honeymoon this time, it seems fitting that we look ahead and behind. Knowing the periodic Marxist inebriation to be expected of one partner and the whilom anti-red frigidity of the other, can we expect the honeymoon to last? Did Jimmy Carter and Deng Xiaoping tie a permanent knot or just begin another cycle in a love-hate relationship? Can the Chinese Revolution and the American Happening settle down together?

We figured in China's revolution during Mao's lifetime, from 1893 to 1976. In 1899–1900 we announced the Open Door, after the imperialist powers were already inside, and in 1912 we applauded the Chinese Republic's sudden attempt at parliamentary government, which didn't work. When China in 1923 opted for party dictatorship, we blamed the reds and eventually backed the anti-red party dictatorship of Chiang Kai-shek with his Wellesley wife and her Harvard brother. Mao later called us imperialist exploiters who backed "feudal reaction," by which he meant private property, special privilege, and elitism. Today we are again becoming privileged tourists and foreign investors who help Chinese modernizers create a new technological elite. Will history booby-trap us again?

This chapter comments on the presentations in *Chinese Economy Post-Mao, A Compendium of Papers,* vol. 1: *Policy and Performance,* printed for the Joint Economic Committee, Congress of the United States, November 9, 1978 (Washington, D.C.: Government Printing Office, 1978); in Chi Hsin, *The Case of the Gang of Four: With First Translation of Teng Hsiao-p'ing's "Three Poisonous Weeds"* (Hong Kong: Cosmos Books, n.d.); in Chi Hsin, *Teng Hsiao-p'ing: A Political Biography* (Hong Kong: Cosmos Books, n.d.), and in similar works. The essay appeared under the title "The New Two China Problem" in the *New York Review of Books,* March 8, 1979. Reprinted with permission from the *New York Review of Books.* Copyright © 1979 Nyrev, Inc.

Chou En-lai and Deng Xiaoping's program for modernization of industry, agriculture, science and technology, and defense is the latest revolutionary solution to China's age-old dilemma of how to govern the villages from the cities. The villages today contain 800 million people, the cities 200 million. By the year 2000, whether or not the Four Modernizations are completed, China's villagers are likely to total 1 billion, her city dwellers perhaps 300 million. Food and government will still be major problems. Americans more accustomed to farmsteads than to villages, whose countryside has generally disappeared into suburbs, can only try to imagine China's situation. The press of numbers creates complexities of economy, government, and values, including human rights, that are all very strange to us.

If we repeat our experience of the 1930s with Nationalist China, trading, investing, educating, and touring mainly in the cities, we can again be startled, embattled, and embittered by what comes out of the villages. China's farming people are not going to disappear like ours into urban centers. They were there in their villages before America began and will no doubt outlast us. The modern revolution is only beginning to reach them. Now that the Chou-Deng program seeks our investment of technology in training, equipment, and joint ventures, we must get our minds out of the familiar cities like Canton, Shanghai, and Peking and into the less known countryside. To help China blindly, knowing only what we are told in English, unaware of what our Chinese friends are up against, is a prescription for another American disaster in China reminiscent of the 1940s.

Having got beyond our thirty-year-old Two Chinas problem by agreeing that Taiwan is a self-governing, armed province over which Peking has latent sovereignty, we now face another Two Chinas, urban and rural. The Chinese Revolution, not yet finished, is really two revolutions, one social and one technological, that sometimes coincide and sometimes conflict. This is what produces the policy zigzags that always amaze us. They are built into the revolutionary process like "walking on two legs," as the man said.

Mao Tse-tung's social revolution aimed to liberate the villagers from second-class citizenship, ignorance, and want. It tried to wipe out the old ruling-class elite of privileged literati, officials, merchants, landlords, and city-dwelling exploiters in general. But mobilizing peasants for this egalitarian purpose inevitably created a great cult of Mao, something like a folk religion, and his latter-day followers led by the so-called Gang of Four wound up as anti-intellectual dogmatists. With "politics in command" they attacked "bourgeois tendencies" like Calvinists routing out original sin. They decried material incentives as unworthy of true socialism. The result was a failure to educate or to produce, which led to an economic stagnation and another shift of course once the Gang was thrown out of power.

Under Deng Xiaoping the other revolution, aimed at applying modern technology to all aspects of Chinese life, now has its day and opportunity. We must help it to succeed, but how far it succeeds and how long it lasts as Peking's dominant policy will depend to some degree on how we do our part. Foreigners of every stripe have always found their counterparts in China. Our opium traders found Chinese opium distributors, our missionaries found Chinese devoted to good works. Even without the help of rip-off specialists in our General Services Administration, Chinese purchasers in capitalist America will truly be in enemy territory. To sup with us, they will need long chopsticks. Even the ten-dollar bills of eleemosynary tourists in China's new thousand-room hotels will be corrupting. With all due respect to one of America's inexpugnable claims to fame, we may also wonder whether Coca-Cola can really hit the spot in Honan province. In summer Shanghai, yes, but will it increase crop acreage in Linhsien, or irrigate more than the purchaser?

In the midst of plans for steel, coal, and oil production to build up industry, we have to wear bifocals that can also keep in view the rural 800 million. They have doubled in numbers since 1949 but are still bone poor. If the new city elite that we help to train should lose touch with the villages, Mao's ghost may well appear and cry "Remember me!" in more than one rural hamlet. Literacy and transistors are spreading expectations among the most cohesive and the largest bloc of people ever to appear on earth. Deng Xiaoping's program for a controlled chain reaction in the Chinese countryside has its dangers. We can expect in ten or twenty years to be feeding China's cities in exchange for consumer goods we cannot produce competitively. But this symbiosis will be with the modern international fringe of China, a mere 200 or 300 million, while the billion farmers of the Chinese countryside, still poor, may be mobilizing anew. In short, we have reason to study more than China's technological needs, appreciate more than the tourist cuisine, and offer more than audience enthusiasm for the Chinese people's great achievements. They have troubles too, and in the global future we cannot escape a connection with them.

Current publications reflect the range of these problems and of Western concerns about them. Some of these books suggest why so many Chinese officials regard foreign China specialists as the most dispensable people. At the moment they must prefer the Western economists to the Western sociologists.

Where Mao urged class struggle as the means of changing consciousness and values, Deng drives today for material production. His program was worked out at conferences in 1975 and was stated in three documents that the Gang of Four attacked as the Three Poisonous Weeds. The general policy statement quotes Chairman Mao in every paragraph, while the industrial development statement is a no-nonsense, rather concrete forecast of lines now being pursued.

Overall, the People's Republic in material terms has done very well. Gross national product has grown about 5.5 percent annually as a whole, and 9.0 percent in industry—rates that we can envy. *If* politics can remain stable and *if* military costs can be restrained, the prospects are bright for a continued slow rise in living standards. But this will not happen of itself and several things may impede it—not only political turmoil or a military buildup but also bad weather or natural disaster like the great Tangshan earthquake of 1976.

One critical problem is that China has run out of crop land. Leveling and combining fields, terracing mountains, reclaiming wasteland are all meeting diminishing returns. Some of the plans for creating new land will boggle the American mind—for example, farming a riverbed by putting the river in a tunnel underneath it. The hand work involved in cutting and carrying the stone for such a river tunnel is the same cheap labor that built the Great Wall, labor that is still the major resource in the country and still low in productivity without more capital equipment. Deng's program for farm mechanization aims mainly to free labor for the rural small-scale industries that are beginning to provide cement, chemicals, iron, power, machinery, and consumer goods for local consumption in the countryside. By American or Soviet standards these small plants are of poor quality and uneconomic. But industry has to go to the villages, and the economy of mass production in central cities must be forgone because no feasible transport system could possibly deliver the goods to 800 million consumers. The villages have to industrialize in situ.

China is so vast in people that statistics require a double take. For instance, China is fourth in the world in primary energy production (after the United States, USSR, and Saudi Arabia), yet her per capita modern energy consumption ranks close to 100th place among the world's 175 countries. Still, China's proportions are formidable: armed forces of 3.5 million, the world's third largest air force, the third biggest nonmilitary aid program, to which one can add twenty-four thousand Chinese technicians sent to the Third World, and the largest machine-building industry—a great power in so many ways. Yet because of numbers the individual's living standard remains lower than we can imagine. Great China may thrive statistically, but the tiny Chinese individual must eke things out.

The basic problem is that while industry has built up rapidly, grain production in the countryside has grown only about 3.0 or 3.5 percent a year. It has barely kept ahead of population growth at 1.8 to 2.0 percent. The agrarian product left over for commercial and industrial use and for export to earn foreign exchange has been very thin. Plans call for 4.5 percent annual growth in grain production, even though from 1964 to 1974 the rate was less than 3.0 percent, and no other major grain producer has been able to maintain a rate of 4.5 percent growth. New fertilizer plants coming "on stream," as the economists so vividly put it, will help. Another tactic in the struggle for grain is to intensify land use by raising not merely two but three crops a year. Our economic analysts, however, see this multiple cropping as a doctrine in need of cost analysis. It requires such early-ripening seeds and so much more labor, fertilizer, and irrigation that it may in fact be uneconomic.

Meanwhile Deng's staccato series of deals for Japanese trucks, British planes, French reactors, German chemicals, and American hotel chains and oil technology—all to be financed with foreign help—has abandoned the Maoist creed of self-reliance. In the re-

sidual Maoist view he also reverses the Cultural Revolution, re-
pudiates Marxism, revives factory "despotism" under one-man
management, reinstates a concern for profit, opposes egalitarianism, and exploits the peasant masses in order to consolidate the
power of the state through the Four Modernizations.

From all this we get a picture of material/technological progress
that seems downright affluent in urban China. But rural China is
a different scene, where the Deng reforms enable some peasants to
get rich but others to grow poor. If the poor should ever outnum-
ber the rich by too high a ratio, flames might shoot up from the
currently burnt-out embers of Maoism. China has had peasant
rebellions before: we shall do well to keep rural China in view.

26

Parallels and Problems

China and America may be on converging paths as we both pursue our modernizations. But the remarkable parallels in our experience since the 1960s are superficial compared with the difference in our circumstances. China cannot develop on our model. The Chinese yearning for American things and ways, which many Americans will encounter in times to come, is an aspect of Chinese life that needs to be kept in a well-informed perspective, lest we mistake it for a wave of the future.

China's speed of change puts a premium on the observer's mental agility and historical memory. Thus the pragmatism espoused by Deng Xiaoping in recent years harks back not to Mao but to the two-year visit of John Dewey to lecture in China in 1919–1921, and to the reformist approach ("bit by bit, drop by drop") then espoused by the Hu Shih wing of the May Fourth movement. Hu Shih, Dewey's student, translated for him and inveighed against ideological "isms" and the violent means they sanctioned. The Marxist-Leninist Ch'en Tu-hsiu wing of the May Fourth movement did not succeed in founding the Chinese Communist Party until June 1921, just as Dewey was returning to America. By the 1940s violent revolution of course seemed essential to inaugurate the new order, but when Mao called for it again in his Cultural Revolution of the late 1960s, things went too far. The subsequent reaction against it in favor of gradual pragmatic reform happily puts China in better tune with the United States. The problems of modern growth that have us by the throat are threat-

This chapter is based in part on a review of Orville Schell's *Watch Out for the Foreign Guests!*, which appeared as "Drop by Drop" in the *New York Review of Books*, April 16, 1981. Reprinted with permission from the *New York Review of Books*. Copyright © 1981 Nyrev, Inc.

ening to strangle China too. We exchange delegations to consult about it. Consultation is possible because, at least insofar as U.S.-Chinese relations are concerned, neither the Chinese nor the Americans suffer at the moment from the fevers of ideological righteousness that have fitfully accompanied our modernizations.

In 1966 we Americans were on our last ideological binge, typically as far off as possible in Vietnam, while the Chinese were having theirs more cheaply at home in Mao's Cultural Revolution. These two fevers burned simultaneously (and very nearly wrecked us both) for most of a decade: 1965–1973 for our crusade in Vietnam, 1966–1976 for Mao's crusade in China. Were they connected? Undoubtedly.

Note first the intellectual limitations of the patriotic leaders on both sides. After the bitter and open Sino-Soviet split of 1960, American leaders who still believed in 1965 that the Soviets and Chinese were a monolithic juggernaut needed a mental examination. They can be forgiven for not knowing the record of Vietnam's ancient hostility to Chinese control, since none of us had ever heard of Vietnam until World War II. After the example of Japan's, Russia's, and even Korea's modernization by foreign borrowing, Chinese leaders who proudly believed China could meet its modern problems in an antiforeign, anti-intellectual isolation, by rapidly reinventing the wheel and the steam engine while changing class structure through repeating Mao's thoughts, also deserved to be tested for their grasp of reality. Mao had found his firmest conviction of reality, of course, in the hillside cave-houses of Yenan.

These intellectual limitations had stronger effect because the leaders on both sides were prisoners of ideology. Both had found cohesion at home in the 1950s by teaching themselves to fear the menace of foreign "communism" and of foreign "imperialism," respectively. They were cognate evils, each seen on the other side as a pervasive menace that must be met by a new birth of righteousness. American GIs bombing villages in Vietnam, Red Guards pillorying intellectuals in China—each nastiness sanctioned the other. Only practical common sense and our mutual disasters in Korea restrained each side from sending troops to meet on the ground in North Vietnam.

After Mao and LBJ had committed themselves to their respective crusades in the late 1960s and met frustration, the parallelism in the experience of China and the United States grew less distinct. No doubt the fall of President Nixon in 1975 and of the Gang of Four in 1976 shared some overtones. At any rate, in 1987 we seem for the moment less fevered on both sides, more at sea, only craving a return from somewhere of that ennobling and reassuring sense of righteousness that makes a national crusade possible.

Orville Schell reports on China's transition from Maoist fervor gone astray under the Gang of Four to Deng's pragmatism of the Four Modernizations. He was one of a small group of American student radicals privileged in 1975 to work in the fields at Mao's national shrine to collective agriculture, the Tachai (Dazhai) Brigade in the loess country of Shansi province west of Peking. (Tachai is now a Lourdes manqué, condemned as having been a fraud.) Since Mao's death in 1976 Schell has been back to Peking and Shanghai three times, running into disaffected Chinese who have talked more and more freely. Their talk makes him wonder, "What ever happened to Mao's revolution?"

Instead of a consul general's report balancing all the factors, Schell offers a series of impressions from personal contact: peasant children at Tachai suddenly seduced into consumerism by a Polaroid camera; disco life and the most feasible of all consumerism, prostitution, at a Peking cafe; would-be Americanized youths riding mopeds in Shanghai; the charming daughter of an official, who spent six years farming in Mongolia and four in a factory before getting into college; an old gentleman in Shanghai who once worked for a foreign firm and was jailed for it; and the new free market in Dairen. The question is the degree to which such Chinese on the alienated urban fringe represent an infection among their countrymen whose consumerist hopes may lead to explosive frustration.

Among these vignettes from the PRC, Schell interlards his journalist's impressions of Deng's visit to Washington, Atlanta, Houston, and Los Angeles, where the American media showed our material gimmicks and crass consumerism for beaming back to China's new TV network. Schell pictures a modernizing America, so free as to lack self-discipline, offering its cultural chaos to a proud but envious modernizing China that cannot afford to buy it and wants no more than selected parts of it in any case.

Schell's vignettes abound in symbolism. Deng's patting a new yellow LTD as it comes off the Ford assembly line in Hapeville, Georgia, signals to his watching countrymen that it is "again permissible to aspire toward Western luxuries; again proper to exalt technocrats." Schell sees a breakthrough at the rodeo in Simonton, Texas: as celebrities, Deng and his entourage have been besieged by Americans wanting things from them. But the Texans at the rodeo, "instead of trying to ingratiate themselves like everyone else," are simply their "normal boisterous and hospitable selves" with no designs at all. It makes for mutual acceptance, which can include the obvious point that our two countries face a host of common problems on which we may be able to help each other.

The acceptance of ever more extensive American contact is, however, a dream that seems to have already faded in China. The gross incongruities in styles of life point up the need to go slow in our getting together. Neither Orville Schell nor any of his Chinese friends see how the Americanization of China can go on unchecked. His friends prefer to escape China and come to America. Personal automobiles cannot become a necessary tool of life among a billion Chinese. Nor can the Chinese afford the conceits that some of us cherish, for example that a fetus before five months is already a person, or that handguns are commodities to buy and sell in the marketplace like any other. American profligacy is beyond their material capacity. Meanwhile our type of modern legality and litigation has not yet got very far in taking precedence over China's traditional morality.

Deng and his successors must try to keep the postrevolutionary growth damped down to the level of a controlled reaction. Sociological research, for example, is part of the modernization of science, but that fact does not mean that American sociologists can have the run of the Chinese countryside. Everything about America has side effects likely to raise the level of hope and frustration for individual Chinese. Since the PRC's billion people are the world's greatest pool of talent, too many American stimuli can touch off strains that may lead to explosions. We are too easily aggressive. Rather than let the Harlem Globetrotters recruit in China, we must wait for the Chinese basketball administration to field its own team of seven-foot-tall ball handlers.

Let us not forget that China has been until very recently a dominant majority civilization in its own part of the globe. It has therefore been slow to take on the task of being a developing minority society in today's international world. America as a society of immigrants and developers may keep on trying to expand its relations with China. But China's leaders are constantly tempted, as Mao was, to keep the outside world at arm's length. This idea is enforced by the combined pride and poverty of a billion people with a powerful sense of identity and of material needs.

The alienation from Mao's post-1957 thought that Schell finds in his marginal people also seems widespread among Chinese intellectuals, beginning with the many victims of the Cultural Revolution, that hysterical process by which the later revolutionaries tried to destroy the earlier revolutionaries. Mao's leadership in thus bombarding the party headquarters and destroying the party itself cast him in the role of tyrant. But it created a major dilemma of legitimacy for the new team under Deng. When Stalin was exposed as a tyrant, the Soviets could still bow to Lenin as the founding father. But Mao is for China's revolution both founding father and, as now exposed, tyrant. The horror stories of destruction of things, people, and values during the Cultural Revolution accumulate day by day. The Deng regime now confronts the problem of how to avoid throwing out Mao's entire legacy along with the Gang of Four.

This the Chinese will not do, nor would it be justified. But their need to limit the Americanizing aspects of China's modernization is plainly necessary not only for simple reasons of cost but also because of that more subtle xenophobic heritage expressed in Schell's title, *Watch Out for the Foreign Guests!* In short, pragmatism has its limits. The approach to the United States cannot be all-out.

Afterword

Two things may be said about the books considered in the preceding chapters. First, they are mainly concerned with China as an intellectual aspect of the United States. They treat the work in China of American merchants, diplomats, missionaries, and soldiers—or else the encounters of American reporters with Chinese life and revolution. Second, they all confront in some fashion the difference in the status of the individual in the two societies.

No doubt this concern for what we now call human rights reflects an ardent American effort to promote them abroad as part of safeguarding them at home. The fact is that in this country the individual's old freedoms seem to be in a losing battle with technology, which constantly finds new ways to integrate the American individual into the computerized, homogenized consumer society and economy. In the missionary century after 1830, God was by no means wholly regnant in American life, and missions abroad were considered vital to the health of the struggling church at home. Our latter-day nondenominational cause of human rights is in the same spot today: it must be supported at home and abroad simultaneously.

How far this American faith puts us at odds with a China that has usually kept the individual more collectivized as part of family and community is a very slippery question in need of painstaking analysis. On the level of individual conduct we must note the Confucian emphasis on duties as against the Western stress on rights. To what degree did the Confucian belief in the perfectibility of the superior person resonate with Christian ideals? To what degree can the Confucian humanism of the traditional elite become a vital part of China's new mass culture? Is a Confucian communism actually emerging in China?

However this may turn out, we can expect the Chinese consensus to be conservative, favoring the interests of state and society over those of the individual. Thus in the late 1980s we shall probably find ourselves still on one side in China's ongoing struggle between party authority and individual self-expression.

In 1987 this conflict took the form of student demonstrations for "democracy," however defined, which touched off a crackdown on tendencies toward "bourgeois liberalization" condemned by some as "spiritual pollution" from abroad.

Naturally those Americans interested in China are likely to sympathize with China's intellectuals, not her commissars. Lest we pose the issue in terms even more simplistic than usual, however, we should note certain background factors that may give the edge to the commissars.

The first is the acceleration of change in China. The mid-1980s saw changes that in the 1970s were inconceivable except as fantasies: rural entrepreneurs really getting rich; workers finding cracks in their iron rice-bowls as job tenure was geared more closely to performance; intellectuals debating the merits of political systems; writers and artists experimenting. Tremendous vitality filled the Chinese cultural scene, as though creative capacities bottled up for decades were now finding outlet. Chinese talent was also taking its place in the international world. This creative growth, however, led to an accumulation of problems. In production and trade, for example, personal initiatives fostered corruption. Modifying the command economy with certain features of a market economy was not easy. Importing foreign technology and capital through joint ventures met limitations. Deng Xiaoping's Open Door had brought tremendous results, but after eight years of great activity in economic reform the student demands for political reform threatened the CCP monopoly of power. The Maoist-minded among more than forty million party members (half of whom entered the party during the Cultural Revolution) could be expected to seek a change of line.

The factor most difficult to appraise was the mood and situation of the Chinese Communist Party. How far could it relax its dictatorial controls and still retain power? Could it actually move from rule to Maoist morality to rule by constitutional legal process? Given the righteousness of any revolution and the conformity demanded by collective life in villages, to say nothing of a communist party, one would not expect much tolerance of dissidents. In Mao's China political deviance had been a treasonous crime far more serious than theft or homicide. It was not possible to separate policy from patriotism and tolerate a loyal opposition. Today the old Confucian tenets seem imbedded in the CCP system: that one rules by virtue of wisdom and rectitude; that theory and practice are a unity, policies a form of conduct manifesting one's character, and attacks on policy therefore attacks on the ruling power. Consequently even today the People's Republic has many political prisoners undergoing reform through labor. There is a general prohibition of torture as such, but Chinese conceptions of political offenses, judicial procedures, and labor reform permit the lack of habeas corpus; unremitting pressure to confess; the use of humiliation, short rations, solitary confinement, handcuffs, and peer group struggle sessions to secure compliant thought and conduct. This underdevelopment of the judicial system partly explains why Chinese students call so intensely for "democracy."

Of course China's small elite of students are not simple counterparts of American students. On the contrary, they see themselves as inheritors of the ancient tradition of government by scholars. As potential officials they are custodians of the nation's welfare, circumstantially required even if by default to assume a political posture. The fact that a selected cohort of students from China excel in American academic life does not change the hard conditions they may face at work in China. Their concerns and ours can hardly be identical.

Nevertheless, now more than ever, we Americans are playing a role, perhaps for the good, in China's development.

INDEX

Missionaries (*continued*)
 Catholic, 15, 29; and emancipation of
 Chinese women, 24, 26, 28; journals,
 25–26. *See also* Hersey, John
Miyazaki Toten, 44; *My Thirty-Three
 Years' Dream,* 43–45, 46, 48
Modernization, 145, 151, 161, 195,
 201–202, 203–205; and social revolu-
 tion, 93; and Confucianism, 110. *See
 also* Deng Xiaoping
Mongols, 20, 33, 35, 36, 132, 182
Montgomery, Sir Bernard, 60
Morrison, G. E., 36, 38
Morrison, Robert, 29
Morse, H. B.: *International Relations of
 the Chinese Empire,* 5
Mott, John R., 27, 30
Mutsu Munemitsu: *Kenkenroku,* 43,
 45–48

Nationalism, 3, 6, 11, 12, 24, 126
Nationalists, Chinese, *see* Kuomintang
Nehru, 115, 116, 117, 118–119, 120,
 121, 124
New Yorker, 29
New York Times, 68, 70, 185
*New York Times Report from Red
 China,* 67n, 68–70
Nimitz, Chester, 61
Nixon, Richard, 70, 107–108, 129, 203;
 visit to China (1972), 66, 67, 114,
 125, 127, 128, 131; and Chou En-lai,
 107, 131, 138
Nuclear power, 125, 137

Office of Strategic Services (OSS), 60
Office of War Information (OWI), 60,
 149
Okinawa, 138
One Billion (Mathews and Mathews),
 184n, 192–194
Open Door doctrine, 6, 12, 19, 20, 22,
 33, 195
Opium trade, 4, 13–17, 19, 197
Opium War, 13–17, 130
Orwell, George, 181, 182
Outer Mongolia, 116
Oxford University, Bodleian Library, 40,
 42

Palmerston, Lord, 14, 19
Pasqualini, Jean, *see* Bao Ruo-wang
Pearl Harbor, 51, 53, 61
Peking, 35–37, 97, 127–128, 170, 196;
 missionaries in, 24; foreign community of, 36–37, 40, 41, 51; visitors to,
 50–51, 96, 107, 136–137, 177, 179;
 in 1970s, 67, 70, 71, 99, 125, 181;
 T'ien-an Men Square, 88, 154, 181–
 182; U.S. correspondents in, 185, 203
Peking Gazette, 25
Peking Union Medical College, 42
P'eng Te-huai, 146
People's Republic of China (PRC), 13,
 69, 76, 89, 125; tourism, 7, 180–181,
 185, 195, 197, 198; peasantry, 9, 187,
 196, 197, 200; U.S. reporters in, 68–
 70, 97, 177, 184–194, 208; social organization, 70, 76, 108; political
 expression, 75, 76, 77, 208; technology, 75, 76, 110, 131, 208; education,
 76, 110, 146, 160, 162; de Gaulle's
 recognition of, 77; and Chinese tradition, 88; politics compared with U.S.,
 92, 93; and human rights, 95, 143,
 207; view of Americans, 97, 112;
 prostitution, 97, 203; sex, 98, 192–
 193; performing arts, 101–103; and
 Third World, 126, 127, 159; Ninth
 Party Congress (1969), 127; and international trade, 133; vs. Taiwan,
 134; and civil liberties, 143, 196; intelligentsia, 161, 164, 180, 183, 193,
 208; meritocracy, 165, 166; material
 achievements, 183, 198–200; control
 system, 187–188; overpopulation,
 188–189, 193, 196, 199; dissent, 193,
 208, 209; city vs. countryside, 196–
 200; economy, 198–200, 208; grain
 production, 199; student demonstrations (1987), 208, 209. *See also* Mao
 Tse-tung
Pershing, John J., 57, 58, 59
Philippines, 57, 58, 59, 60, 61, 138
Portuguese, 131
PRC, *see* People's Republic of China
Prisoner of Mao (Bao and Chelminski),
 75n, 78–85

Quemoy, 146, 155